Cakes, Pastries and Bread

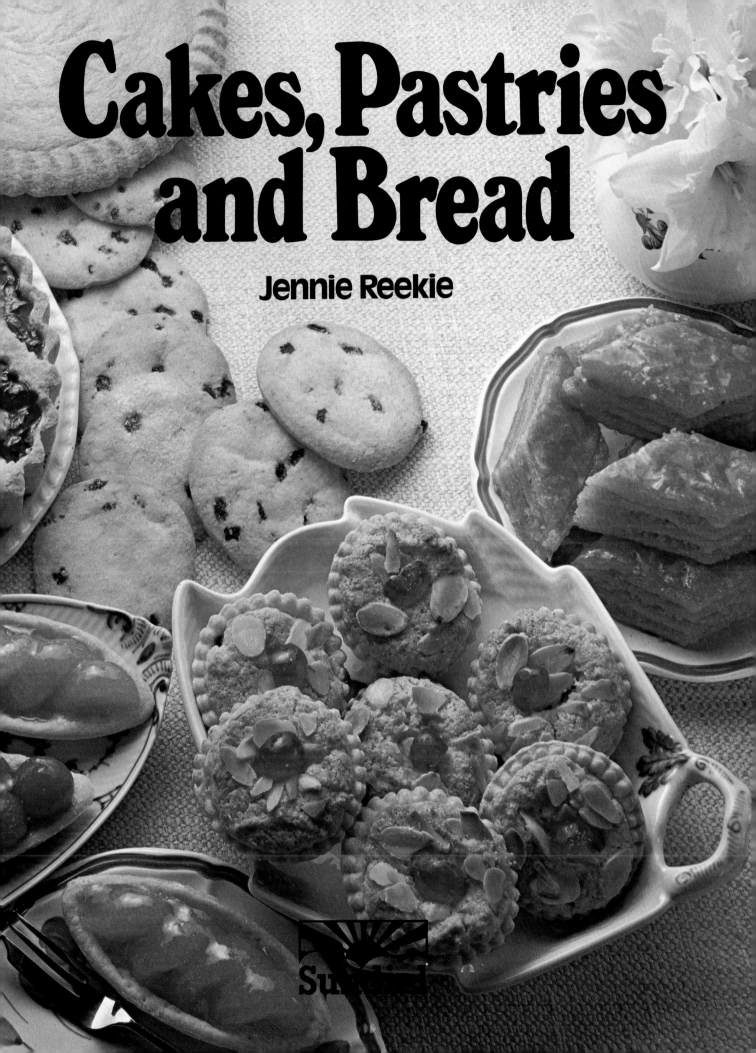

Cakes, Pastries and Bread

Jennie Reekie

Sundial

Contents

First published in 1977 by Sundial Books Limited
59 Grosvenor Street, London W1
Twelfth impression, 1981

© 1977 Hennerwood Publications Limited

ISBN 0 904230 44 9

Printed in Hong Kong

Introduction

Baking is a most satisfying kind of cookery, and there is a deep sense of achievement in making one's own bread, cakes and scones. Nowadays it is far less time-consuming – an important aspect for the growing number of working housewives – for modern methods and equipment have considerably reduced the preparation times needed for cakes and breads.

A small electric mixer cuts out much wearisome beating and whisking. Non-stick tins and baking sheets need not be lined with greased grease-proof paper (so ignore the lining instructions given in the recipes if you are fortunate enough to have these). Most dried fruit is pre-washed and does not need washing and drying, and soft margarines mean that you need not cream fat and sugar together but can simply beat all ingredients together in a bowl.

Most cakes, breads and scones also freeze extremely well, so that if you have a freezer you can make up large batches and freeze them in polythene bags or in double-thickness foil. This means that you can devote one day to doing the baking for almost a month's supply.

Iced and decorated cakes are best open frozen so that the decorations are not spoilt, then wrapped in foil or polythene and replaced in the freezer. When you wish to use a frozen cake remove it from the freezer, take off the wrapping and place the cake on a plate to defrost at room temperature or overnight in a refrigerator.

Even if you have not done much baking before you need not buy an enormous selection of

different-sized tins. Many of the cakes are baked in 18–20 cm (7–8 inch) tins, and you can build up your collection gradually. For occasional bread-making a loaf tin is not essential, as the dough can just as easily be made into a round or a cottage loaf and placed on a greased and floured baking sheet. But if you start making bread regularly you will probably want to buy at least a couple of tins.

Should you want to bake a cake in a round tin instead of a square one as given in a recipe – or vice versa – the round tin must be a little larger; i.e. for an 18 cm (7 inch) square tin you will need a 20 cm (8 inch) round one. Unfortunately not all tins are of standard size and may often be a little larger or smaller than the sizes given, so you may have to use your own judgment as to which size of tin to choose. If you are making up the mixture

by metric measurements take a slightly smaller size of tin rather than a larger one, as these measurements have been rounded down to the nearest 25 grams, which means that you have slightly less mixture.

Always follow manufacturer's instructions for cleaning and storing tins, especially non-stick ones, as these are quite expensive and you do not want to ruin the surface by scratching it.

This book is essentially about baking, and does not go into great detail about the icing and decorating of cakes for this is itself a specialist subject. But the book does cover all main aspects of baking – cakes, scones and teabreads, yeasted breads, pastries, biscuits and cookies – and all readers should find plenty of recipes which they will enjoy making and which their family and friends will enjoy eating.

In the following pages you will find all the basic cake recipes such as Victoria Sandwich, Whisked Sponge, Rock Cakes, Madeira Cake, Dundee Cake and Gingerbread, as well as rather more unusual recipes like Swedish Cardamom Cake and Swiss Carrot Cake.

Sponge cakes are the most popular cakes of all, especially with small children who often do not like dried fruit, nuts and cherries. Three basic recipes have been given: Victoria Sandwich, the classic butter sponge; the fatless Whisked Sponge; and Never-fail Sponge, which is fool-proof for inexperienced bakers.

There are many different reasons why cakes can fail. One of the most usual is because in a creamed mixture the butter and sugar have not been sufficiently beaten together. Again the egg may have been added too quickly causing the mixture to curdle. Although a cake which has curdled will still rise, it will not usually rise as high as it should. It is also essential to fold in the flour in a figure-of-eight movement, using a metal spoon, and not stir it in, as stirring knocks out a great deal of the air which you have incorporated in the beating or whisking.

The oven temperature is also very important and it is a good idea to check your oven from time to time with an oven thermometer. If you bake a cake at too high a temperature it will not rise properly as the top forms a crust which stops the mixture underneath from expanding. Equally if a particular cake is baked at too low a temperature there will not be sufficient heat to make it rise. Most cakes should be baked in the centre of the oven. If you are baking cakes in sandwich tins you can either put the cakes side by side on the same oven shelf if there is enough room, or put them directly underneath each other and allow the lower cake 2–3 minutes longer. You will find from experience which is the better with your oven.

Some of the easiest and quickest cakes to prepare are those made by the melting method, when the fat and sugar are melted together and added to the dry ingredients, for example as in a gingerbread. These cakes usually keep well in airtight containers for about two weeks, and indeed improve with keeping. Rich fruit cakes also keep well and are better if they are left to mature, so there is no need to freeze this kind of cake. Ideally one should make a Christmas cake around the beginning of November, so that it has about six weeks to mature before you put on the almond paste and royal icing. When making a rich fruit cake brandy can be added to the mixture before it is cooked, but it does evaporate during cooking and a stronger brandy flavour is achieved if it is added afterwards, as in the recipe on page 24.

Victoria sandwich

Victoria sandwich

Metric	Imperial
100 g self-raising flour	4 oz self-raising flour
100 g butter or margarine	4 oz butter or margarine
100 g caster sugar	4 oz caster sugar
2 standard eggs, beaten	2 large eggs, beaten
$\frac{1}{4}$ teaspoon vanilla essence	$\frac{1}{4}$ teaspoon vanilla essence

To finish:
Jam, butter cream or
whipped cream
Caster or icing sugar

To finish:
Jam, butter cream or
whipped cream
Caster or icing sugar

Cooking Time: 20–25 minutes
Oven: 180°C, 350°F, Gas Mark 4

Grease 2 × 15–18 cm (6–7 in) sandwich tins and line the bases with greased greaseproof paper. Sieve the flour. Cream the butter and sugar together in a bowl, either by hand with a wooden spoon or with an electric beater, until the mixture is very light and fluffy. Gradually beat in the eggs, blended with the vanilla essence, adding a spoonful of the sieved flour with the last amount. Carefully fold in the sieved flour.

Divide the mixture between the two sandwich tins and bake in a moderate oven for 20–25 minutes or until the cakes are golden brown and spring back when lightly pressed. Remove from the oven, leave to cool for a couple of minutes, then turn out on to a wire rack and leave until quite cold.

Sandwich the cakes together with jam or cream and sprinkle the top with a little sugar.

Variations

Orange or lemon cake: Omit the vanilla essence and cream 2 × 5 ml spoons (2 teaspoons) finely grated orange or lemon rind with the butter and sugar.

Quick Mix Victoria Sandwich: Use 100 g (4 oz) soft margarine. Put into a mixing bowl with the sugar, eggs and vanilla. Sieve in the flour and 1 × 5 ml spoon (1 teaspoon) baking powder and mix all the ingredients together for 1 minute.

Chocolate swiss roll with peppermint cream

Metric

2 standard eggs
50 g caster sugar
50 g self-raising flour,
less 1 × 15 ml spoon
1 × 15 ml spoon cocoa
powder
Extra caster sugar for
dredging

For the filling:
50 g butter
75 g icing sugar, sieved
Few drops peppermint
essence

Imperial

2 large eggs
2 oz caster sugar
2 oz self-raising flour,
less 1 tablespoon
1 tablespoon cocoa
powder
Extra caster sugar for
dredging

For the filling:
2 oz butter
3 oz icing sugar, sieved
Few drops peppermint
essence

Cooking Time: 7–10 minutes
Oven: 200°C, 400°F, Gas Mark 6

Grease an 18 × 28 cm (7 × 11 in) swiss roll tin and line the base and sides with greased greaseproof paper. Whisk the eggs and sugar together until they are light and creamy and the whisk leaves a trail when it is lifted out. Sieve in the flour and cocoa, then fold into the mixture. Turn into the tin and level off.

Bake in a moderately hot oven for 7–10 minutes until the cake springs back when lightly pressed. Turn out on to a piece of greaseproof paper dredged with caster sugar. Trim off the edges and quickly roll up the swiss roll, keeping it wrapped in the greaseproof paper. Allow to cool.

Cream the butter and icing sugar together, then beat in the peppermint essence. Unroll the cake, removing the greaseproof paper, spread with the peppermint butter cream, then re-roll. Dredge the outside of the roll with caster sugar before serving.

Simple sponge cake; Whisked sponge; Chocolate swiss roll with peppermint cream

Simple sponge cake

Metric	Imperial
175 g caster sugar	7 oz caster sugar
3 standard eggs	3 large eggs
50 g butter	2 oz butter
2 × 15 ml spoons water	3 tablespoons water
½ teaspoon vanilla essence	½ teaspoon vanilla essence
125 g plain flour	5 oz plain flour

To finish:
3 × 15 ml spoons jam	3 tablespoons jam
Icing sugar, sieved	Icing sugar, sieved

Cooking Time: 20–25 minutes
Oven: 190°C, 375°F, Gas Mark 5

Grease 2 × 18 cm (7 in) sandwich tins and line the bases with greased greaseproof paper. Whisk the sugar and eggs together with an electric beater for 10 minutes. Put the butter and water into a small pan and heat gently until the butter has melted. Pour into the whisked mixture with the vanilla essence and whisk just for half a minute. Sieve in the flour and fold into the mixture. Turn into the prepared tins and give each tin a sharp tap to settle the mixture. Bake in a moderately hot oven for 20–25 minutes or until well risen and the cakes spring back when lightly pressed. Leave in the tins for 2–3 minutes, then turn out on to a wire rack to cool. When cold sandwich together with the jam and sprinkle the top with icing sugar.

Whisked sponge

Metric	Imperial
75 g self-raising flour	3 oz self-raising flour
3 standard eggs	3 large eggs
75 g caster sugar	3 oz caster sugar
1 × 15 ml spoon hot water	1 tablespoon hot water

To finish:
3 × 15 ml spoons raspberry or other jam	3 tablespoons raspberry or other jam
Icing sugar, sieved	Icing sugar, sieved

Cooking Time: 15–20 minutes
Oven: 180°C, 350°F, Gas Mark 4

Grease 2 × 18 cm (7 in) sandwich tins and line the bases with greased greaseproof paper. Sieve the flour twice on to a piece of greaseproof paper. Put the eggs and sugar into a bowl (if whisking by hand you must stand the bowl over a pan of hot water, but this is not essential if using an electric mixer). Whisk until very thick and creamy and the whisk leaves a trail when lifted out of the mixture.
Sprinkle the flour over the top and carefully fold into the mixture with a metal spoon. Finally fold in the hot water. Divide the mixture between the tins. Bake in a moderate oven for 15–20 minutes or until the cakes spring back when lightly pressed. Leave in the tins for 1–2 minutes, then turn out on to a wire rack to cool. When cold, sandwich together with jam and sprinkle icing sugar over.

Madeira cake

Metric	Imperial
200 g plain flour	8 oz plain flour
Pinch of salt	Pinch of salt
1 × 5 ml spoon baking powder	1 teaspoon baking powder
125 g butter or margarine	5 oz butter or margarine
125 g caster sugar	5 oz caster sugar
1 × 5 ml spoon finely grated lemon rind	1 teaspoon finely grated lemon rind
2 standard eggs, lightly beaten	2 large eggs, lightly beaten
4 × 15 ml spoons milk	5 tablespoons milk
Citron peel	Citron peel

Cooking Time: 1 hour   Oven: 180°C, 350°F, Gas Mark 4

Grease a 15 cm (6 in) cake tin and line the base with greased greaseproof paper. Sieve the flour, salt and baking powder. Cream the butter or margarine, sugar and lemon rind until light and fluffy. Beat in the eggs a little at a time. Fold in the flour, then enough milk to give a soft dropping consistency. Turn the mixture into the prepared tin. Bake in a moderate oven for 1 hour or until well risen and golden brown, opening the oven door after 30 minutes to place a slice of citron peel gently on top. Leave in the tin for 5 minutes, then turn out on to a wire rack to cool.

Note : Whole citron peel is not always easily available in grocers and supermarkets, but can usually be obtained from health food shops.

Variations

Replace 25 g (1 oz) of the flour with cornflour or rice flour for a finer texture.

Orange Madeira Cake : Omit the lemon rind and milk and replace with orange rind and orange juice.

Coffee Madeira Cake : Omit the lemon rind and replace with 2 × 15 ml spoons (2 tablespoons) of the milk with strong black coffee.

Caraway Seed Cake : Add 1–2 × 5 ml spoons (1–2 teaspoons) of caraway seeds.

Almond Madeira Cake : Omit the lemon rind, add ½ teaspoon almond essence and sprinkle with flaked almonds before baking.

Coconut and cherry cake

Metric	Imperial
300 g self-raising flour	12 oz self-raising flour
Pinch of salt	Pinch of salt
150 g margarine	6 oz margarine
200 g glacé cherries, quartered	8 oz glacé cherries, quartered
50 g desiccated coconut	2 oz desiccated coconut
150 g caster sugar	6 oz caster sugar
2 standard eggs, lightly beaten	2 large eggs, lightly beaten
125 ml milk	Generous ¼ pint milk

Cooking Time: 1½ hours   Oven: 180°C, 350°F, Gas Mark 4

Well grease a 20 cm (8 in) cake tin and line the base with greased greaseproof paper. Sieve together the flour and salt. Rub in the margarine until the mixture resembles fine breadcrumbs. Toss the cherries in the coconut and add to the mixture with the sugar. Mix lightly. Add the eggs to the mixture with most of the milk. Beat well, then add sufficient extra milk to give a soft dropping consistency. Turn into the prepared tin, level off and bake in a moderate oven for 1½ hours or until well risen and golden brown. Leave in the tin for 5 minutes, then turn out on to a wire rack to cool.

Almond layer cake

Metric	Imperial
4 standard eggs	4 large eggs
100 g caster sugar	4 oz caster sugar
75 g self-raising flour	3 oz self-raising flour
50 g ground almonds	2 oz ground almonds
Few drops almond essence	Few drops almond essence

For the icing:	For the icing:
3 egg whites	3 egg whites
500 g caster sugar	1 lb 2 oz caster sugar
Pinch of salt	Pinch of salt
5 × 15 ml spoons cold water	6 tablespoons cold water
Pinch of cream of tartar	Pinch of cream of tartar
50 g toasted flaked almonds	2 oz toasted flaked almonds

Cooking Time: 20 minutes
Oven: 190°C, 375°F, Gas Mark 5

Grease a roasting tin about 38 × 30 cm (15 × 12 in) and line the base and sides with greased greaseproof paper. Whisk the eggs and sugar until the mixture is thick and creamy and the whisk leaves a trail when it is lifted out. Sieve in the flour and fold into the mixture with the ground almonds and the almond essence. Turn the mixture into the prepared tin and level off. Bake in a moderately hot oven for 20 minutes or until the cake is pale golden and springs back when lightly pressed. Turn out on to a sheet of greaseproof paper and leave to cool. When the cake is cold cut it across into three rectangles.

Put the egg whites, sugar, salt, water and cream of tartar into a bowl and place over a pan of hot water. Beat with a rotary whisk or electric hand beater until the mixture thickens and forms peaks – about 7 minutes. Spread some of the icing on two of the rectangles of cake, sprinkle with some of the almonds and sandwich the layers together. Spread the remainder all over the top and sides of the cake and sprinkle with the remaining almonds. Leave to set for at least an hour in a cool place.

Chocolate and orange layer cake

Metric	Imperial
200 g self-raising flour	8 oz self-raising flour
50 g cocoa powder	2 oz cocoa powder
200 g butter or margarine	8 oz butter or margarine
150 g soft brown sugar	6 oz soft brown sugar
2 × 5 ml spoons finely grated orange rind	2 teaspoons finely grated orange rind
100 g black treacle	4 oz black treacle
4 standard eggs, lightly beaten	4 large eggs, lightly beaten

To finish:	To finish:
200 g butter	8 oz butter
400 g icing sugar, sieved	1 lb icing sugar, sieved
3 × 15 ml spoons orange juice	3 tablespoons orange juice
Chocolate vermicelli	Chocolate vermicelli
Crystallised orange slices	Crystallised orange slices

Cooking Time: 1¼ hours   Oven: 180°C, 350°F, Gas Mark 4

Grease a 20 cm (8 in) cake tin and line the base with greased greaseproof paper. Sieve together the flour and cocoa. Cream the butter or margarine, sugar and orange rind until the mixture is light and fluffy. Beat in the treacle. Gradually beat in the eggs, adding a tablespoon of the sifted flour and cocoa with the last amount. Fold in the remaining flour. Turn into the prepared tin and bake for 1¼ hours or until the cake springs back when lightly pressed. Leave in the tin for 5 minutes, turn out and cool on a wire rack. Store in an airtight tin for 3–4 days before icing, for the cake to mature.

Cream the butter and beat in the icing sugar and orange juice. Cut the cake into 3 rounds. Spread the bottom two with some of the icing, then reassemble the cake. Spread some of the remaining butter icing round the sides of the cake, then roll in chocolate vermicelli. Spread most of the remainder over the top of the cake reserving a little icing to pipe small rosettes round the edge. Decorate with crystallised orange slices or similar decorations.

Glazed honey and almond loaf; Chocolate and orange layer cake; Almond layer cake

Glazed honey and almond loaf

Metric

100 g butter or margarine
75 g caster sugar
2 × 15 ml spoons clear honey
2 standard eggs, lightly beaten
150 g self-raising flour
100 g glacé cherries, halved
50 g blanched almonds, chopped

To finish:

1 × 15 ml spoon clear honey
75 g icing sugar, sieved
50 g glacé cherries, halved
50 g blanched almonds

Imperial

4 oz butter or margarine
3 oz caster sugar
2 tablespoons clear honey
2 large eggs, lightly beaten
6 oz self-raising flour
4 oz glacé cherries, halved
2 oz blanched almonds, chopped

To finish:

1 tablespoon clear honey
3 oz icing sugar, sieved
2 oz glacé cherries, halved
2 oz blanched almonds

Cooking Time: 55 minutes
Oven: 180°C, 350°F, Gas Mark 4

Well grease and flour a 600 g (1½ lb) loaf tin. Cream the butter, sugar and honey until light and fluffy. Gradually beat in the eggs, adding a tablespoon of flour with the last amount. Sieve in the remaining flour and fold into the mixture with the cherries and almonds. Turn into the prepared tin and level off the top. Bake in a moderate oven for 55 minutes or until the loaf is golden brown and a skewer inserted in the centre comes out clean. Leave in the tin for 5 minutes, then remove and cool on a wire rack. When the loaf is quite cold beat the honey into the icing sugar, then add sufficient cold water to give a stiff flowing consistency. Spoon most of the icing over the cake, allowing it to drip down the sides. Arrange the cherries and almonds attractively on top and drizzle a little of the remaining icing over them.

Marble cake

Metric	Imperial
150 g butter or margarine	6 oz butter or margarine
150 g caster sugar	6 oz caster sugar
3 standard eggs, lightly beaten	3 large eggs, lightly beaten
150 g self-raising flour	6 oz self-raising flour
½ teaspoon vanilla essence	½ teaspoon vanilla essence
1 × 15 ml spoon cocoa powder	1 tablespoon cocoa powder
For the butter icing:	For the butter icing:
50 g butter or margarine	2 oz butter or margarine
100 g icing sugar, sieved	4 oz icing sugar, sieved
2 × 5 ml spoons cocoa powder	2 teaspoons cocoa powder
2 × 5 ml spoons warm water	2 teaspoons warm water

Cooking Time: 1 hour   Oven: 180°C, 350°F, Gas Mark 4

Grease an 18 cm (7 in) square cake tin and line the base with greased greaseproof paper. Cream the butter or margarine and sugar until light and fluffy. Gradually beat in the eggs. Sieve in all but 1 × 15 ml spoon (1 tablespoon) of the flour and fold into the mixture. Divide the mixture in half. Fold the vanilla essence and remaining flour into one half and the cocoa powder into the other. Put spoonfuls of the mixture alternately in the prepared tin. Bake in a moderate oven for 1 hour until well risen and golden brown. Leave in the tin for 5 minutes, then turn out on to a wire rack to cool.

Cream the butter or margarine and beat in the icing sugar. Dissolve the cocoa in the water and beat into the creamed mixture. Spread the butter icing over the top of the cake and leave to set. Cut into squares to serve.

Queen cakes

Metric	Imperial
75 g self-raising flour	3 oz self-raising flour
Pinch of salt	Pinch of salt
50 g butter or margarine	2 oz butter or margarine
50 g caster sugar	2 oz caster sugar
1 standard egg, lightly beaten	1 large egg, lightly beaten
2 × 5 ml spoons lemon juice	2 teaspoons lemon juice
50 g currants	2 oz currants
Milk to mix	Milk to mix

Cooking Time: 15–20 minutes
Oven: 190°C, 375°F, Gas Mark 5

Place 9 paper cake cases in patty tins – this helps them to keep their shape – or on a baking sheet. Sieve the flour and salt. Cream the butter or margarine and sugar until light and fluffy. Gradually beat in the egg and lemon juice, adding a tablespoon of the flour with the last amount. Fold in the remaining flour and the currants and add enough milk to mix to a soft, dropping consistency.

Divide the mixture between the cases. Bake in a moderately hot oven for 15–20 minutes until well risen and golden brown.

Makes 9

Children's chocolate faces

Metric	Imperial
100 g self-raising flour, less 1 × 15 ml spoon	4 oz self-raising flour, less 1 tablespoon
1 × 15 ml spoon cocoa powder	1 tablespoon cocoa powder
Pinch of salt	Pinch of salt
100 g butter or margarine	4 oz butter or margarine
100 g caster sugar	4 oz caster sugar
2 standard eggs, lightly beaten	2 large eggs, lightly beaten
To finish:	To finish:
100 g icing sugar, sieved	4 oz icing sugar, sieved
Smarties, hundreds and thousands, silver balls or other cake decorations	Smarties, hundreds and thousands, silver balls or other cake decorations

Cooking Time: 15–20 minutes
Oven: 190°C, 375°F, Gas Mark 5

Place 14–16 paper cake cases in patty tins – this helps them to keep their shape – or on a baking sheet. Sieve the flour, cocoa and salt. Cream the butter or margarine and sugar until light and fluffy. Gradually beat in the eggs, adding a tablespoon of the flour and cocoa with the last amount. Fold in the remaining flour and cocoa. Divide the mixture between the cake cases. Bake in a moderately hot oven for 15–20 minutes. Allow to cool.

Beat enough cold water into the icing sugar to give a thick, flowing consistency. Spoon the icing on to the cakes and decorate with Smarties, hundreds and thousands, silver balls or other cake decorations as in the picture.

Makes 14–16

Marble cake; Children's chocolate faces; Queen cakes; Butterfly cakes

Butterfly cakes

Metric

100 g self-raising flour
Pinch of salt
100 g butter or margarine
100 g caster sugar
2 standard eggs, lightly
beaten

For the filling:
50 g butter
100 g icing sugar, sieved
Vanilla essence

Imperial

4 oz self-raising flour
Pinch of salt
4 oz butter or margarine
4 oz caster sugar
2 large eggs, lightly
beaten

For the filling:
2 oz butter
4 oz icing sugar, sieved
Vanilla essence

Cooking Time: 15–20 minutes
Oven: 190°C, 375°F, Gas Mark 5

Place 14–16 paper cake cases in patty tins – this helps them to keep their shape – or on a baking sheet. Sieve the flour and salt. Cream the butter or margarine and sugar until light and fluffy. Gradually beat in the eggs, adding a tablespoon of the flour with the last amount. Fold in the remaining flour. Divide the mixture between the cake cases and bake in a moderately hot oven for 15–20 minutes or until well risen and golden brown. Allow the cakes to cool.

When quite cold cut a circle from the top of each, using a sharp knife. Cut each of these small circles in half. Cream the butter and beat in the icing sugar and a few drops of vanilla essence. Spoon a little butter cream into the centre of each cake and press two semi-circular pieces into it to look like butterfly wings (or pipe three lines of butter cream with a small rose pipe, and place the 'wings' between them).

Makes 14–16

Orange or lemon butterflies : Beat 1 × 5 ml spoon (1 teaspoon) finely grated orange or lemon rind with the butter and sugar. Add 2 × 5 ml spoons (2 teaspoons) orange or lemon juice to the butter icing.

Frosted walnut cake

Frosted walnut cake

Metric	Imperial
3 standard eggs	3 large eggs
75 g caster sugar	3 oz caster sugar
75 g self-raising flour	3 oz self-raising flour
2 × 15 ml spoons corn oil	2 tablespoons corn oil
100 g walnuts, finely chopped	4 oz walnuts, finely chopped

For the filling:

100 g butter	4 oz butter
150 g icing sugar, sieved	6 oz icing sugar, sieved
½ teaspoon vanilla essence	½ teaspoon vanilla essence
A little milk	A little milk

To finish:

400 g granulated sugar	1 lb granulated sugar
125 ml water	¼ pint water
2 egg whites	2 egg whites
8 walnut halves	8 walnut halves

Cooking Time: 25 minutes
Oven: 180°C, 350°F, Gas Mark 4

Grease 2 × 18 cm (7 in) sandwich tins and line the bases with greased greaseproof paper. Whisk the eggs and sugar until they are thick and the whisk leaves a trail when lifted out of the mixture. Sieve in the flour and fold in, then the corn oil and finally the chopped walnuts. Divide the mixture between the two tins and level off. Bake in a moderate oven for about 25 minutes or until the cakes are pale golden and spring back when lightly pressed. Leave in the tins for 2–3 minutes, then turn out and cool on a wire rack. When the cakes are cold split each one in half to make 4 rounds.

Cream the butter and icing sugar. Beat in the vanilla essence and enough milk to give a mixture which will spread easily. Spread the filling on three of the rounds of cake and reassemble.

Put the sugar and water into a heavy pan. Heat gently until the sugar has dissolved, then boil rapidly to 120°C (250°F) or until the mixture forms a hard ball when dropped into a bowl of cold water. Remove from the heat. Whisk the egg whites until they are very stiff then, still beating, pour in the syrup in a slow, steady stream. Continue beating until the icing is thick enough to spread. Quickly spread the icing all over the top and sides of the cake and decorate the top with walnut halves while the icing is still soft. Leave to set.

Mocha fudge cake

Mocha fudge cake

Metric	Imperial
125 g plain flour	*5 oz plain flour*
25 g cocoa powder	*1 oz cocoa powder*
½ teaspoon salt	*½ teaspoon salt*
2 × 5 ml spoons baking powder	*2 teaspoons baking powder*
125 g soft brown sugar	*5 oz soft brown sugar*
2 standard eggs, separated	*2 large eggs, separated*
6 × 15 ml spoons corn oil	*6 tablespoons corn oil*
5 × 15 ml spoons milk	*5 tablespoons milk*
½ teaspoon vanilla essence	*½ teaspoon vanilla essence*

To finish:

Metric	Imperial
4 × 15 ml spoons chocolate spread	*4 tablespoons chocolate spread*
50 g butter or margarine	*2 oz butter or margarine*
100 g soft brown sugar	*4 oz soft brown sugar*
2–3 × 15 ml spoons coffee essence	*2–3 tablespoons coffee essence*
4–5 × 15 ml spoons milk	*4–5 tablespoons milk*
300 g icing sugar, sieved	*12 oz icing sugar, sieved*
25 g plain chocolate	*1 oz plain chocolate*
Few blanched flaked almonds	*Few blanched flaked almonds*

Cooking Time: 20–30 minutes
Oven: 180°C, 350°F, Gas Mark 4

Well grease 2 × 18–20 cm (7–8 in) sandwich tins and line the bases with greased greaseproof paper. Sieve the flour, cocoa, salt and baking powder into a bowl. Add the sugar. Blend together the egg yolks, oil, milk and vanilla essence. Pour into the centre of the dry ingredients and beat well to form a smooth batter. Whisk the egg whites until they form stiff peaks, then fold into the mixture. Turn into the prepared tins and bake for 20–30 minutes or until the tops spring back when lightly pressed. Leave in the tin for 2–3 minutes, then turn out on to a wire rack to cool. Smooth the chocolate spread over one of the cakes and sandwich the two together.

Put the butter or margarine into a saucepan with the sugar, coffee essence and milk; use the larger quantity of milk with the smaller quantity of coffee essence. Heat gently until the butter has melted and the sugar dissolved. Bring to the boil and boil rapidly for 2 minutes. Remove from the heat and gradually beat in the icing sugar. Beat until the frosting has cooled a little and thickened. Quickly spread over the top and sides of the cake using a palette knife dipped in warm water. Leave for 1 hour to set.

Put the chocolate into a small polythene bag and tie the top with a knot. Stand the bag in a bowl of hot water until the chocolate has melted. Snip off one of the bottom corners and pipe over the top of the cake. Decorate with blanched flaked almonds.

Devil's food cake; Quick-mix chocolate and walnut cake; Marmalade cake

Marmalade cake

Metric	Imperial
150 g butter or margarine	*6 oz butter or margarine*
150 g caster sugar	*6 oz caster sugar*
2 × 5 ml spoons finely grated orange rind	*2 teaspoons finely grated orange rind*
3 standard eggs, separated	*3 large eggs, separated*
250 g self-raising flour	*10 oz self-raising flour*
3 × 15 ml spoons dark chunky marmalade	*3 tablespoons dark chunky marmalade*
50 g chopped mixed peel	*2 oz chopped mixed peel*
4 × 15 ml spoons water	*5 tablespoons water*

For the glacé icing:
100 g icing sugar, sieved
About 1 × 15 ml spoon orange juice
½ orange

For the glacé icing:
4 oz icing sugar, sieved
About 1 tablespoon orange juice
½ orange

Cooking Time: 1¼ hours   Oven: 180°C, 350°F, Gas Mark 4

Grease an 18 cm (7 in) cake tin and line the base with greased greaseproof paper. Cream the butter or margarine, sugar and orange rind until light and fluffy. Beat in the egg yolks, one at a time, then 1 × 15 ml spoon (1 tablespoon) of the sieved flour. Stir in the marmalade, peel and water. Fold in the remaining flour. Whisk the egg whites until they are just stiff, then fold into the mixture. Turn into the prepared tin and bake in a moderate oven for 1¼ hours or until golden brown and firm to the touch. Leave in the tin for 5 minutes, then turn out and cool on a wire rack.

Blend the icing sugar with the orange juice to a thick, flowing consistency. Spoon carefully over the top of the cold cake. Thinly slice the orange and cut each slice into quarters. Arrange in 4 diagonal lines on the cake.

Devil's food cake

Metric	Imperial
150 g plain flour	6 oz plain flour
¼ teaspoon baking powder	¼ teaspoon baking powder
1 × 5 ml spoon bicarbonate of soda	1 teaspoon bicarbonate of soda
50 g cocoa powder	2 oz cocoa powder
200 ml water	7½ fl oz water
100 g butter	4 oz butter
250 g caster sugar	10 oz caster sugar
2 standard eggs, lightly beaten	2 large eggs, lightly beaten
For the butter cream:	For the butter cream:
40 g butter	1½ oz butter
50 g icing sugar, sieved	2 oz icing sugar, sieved
40 g plain chocolate	1½ oz plain chocolate
1 × 5 ml spoon water	1 teaspoon water
For the frosting:	For the frosting:
2 egg whites	2 egg whites
300 g icing sugar, sieved	12 oz icing sugar, sieved
Pinch of salt	Pinch of salt
Pinch of cream of tartar	Pinch of cream of tartar
3 × 15 ml spoons water	4 tablespoons water

Cooking Time: 50 minutes
Oven: 180°C, 350°F, Gas Mark 4

Grease 2 × 20 cm (8 in) sandwich tins and line the bases with greased greaseproof paper. Sieve the flour, baking powder and bicarbonate of soda. Blend the cocoa and water together. Cream the butter, add the sugar and beat until light and fluffy. Gradually beat in the eggs. Fold in the flour alternately with the cocoa mixture. Divide the mixture between the prepared tins and bake in a moderate oven for about 50 minutes or until just firm to the touch. Leave in the tins for 2 minutes, turn out and cool on a wire rack.
Cream the butter and beat in the icing sugar. Melt the chocolate with the water in a basin over a pan of hot water. Beat into the butter and sugar. Use to sandwich the cakes together.
Put the egg whites, sugar, salt, cream of tartar and water into a large bowl. Place over a pan of hot water and whisk with a hand whisk or electric beater until the mixture is thick enough to form peaks – about 7 minutes. Spread all over the top and sides of the cake, forming into swirls with a knife. Leave to set.

Quick-mix chocolate and walnut cake

Metric	Imperial
150 g self-raising flour	6 oz self-raising flour
1 × 5 ml spoon baking powder	1 teaspoon baking powder
Pinch of salt	Pinch of salt
25 g cocoa powder	1 oz cocoa powder
2 × 15 ml spoons warm water	2 tablespoons warm water
150 g soft margarine	6 oz soft margarine
150 g caster sugar	6 oz caster sugar
3 standard eggs	3 large eggs
65 g walnuts, finely chopped	2½ oz walnuts, finely chopped
For the icing:	For the icing:
75 g butter or margarine	3 oz butter or margarine
1 × 15 ml spoon cocoa powder	1 tablespoon cocoa powder
1 × 15 ml spoon warm water	1 tablespoon warm water
200 g icing sugar, sieved	8 oz icing sugar, sieved
25 g walnut halves	1 oz walnut halves

Cooking Time: 35–45 minutes
Oven: 180°C, 350°F, Gas Mark 4

Grease a 28 cm (11 in) cake tin and line the base with greased greaseproof paper. Sieve the flour, baking powder and salt into a bowl. Blend the cocoa with the warm water and add to the bowl with the margarine, sugar, eggs and walnuts. Beat the mixture with a wooden spoon until all the ingredients are well blended, then beat for a further minute. Turn into the prepared tin and bake in a moderate oven for 35–45 minutes or until the cake springs back when lightly pressed. Leave in the tin for 2–3 minutes, turn out on to a wire rack and leave until cold.
For the icing, melt the butter or margarine in a pan. Blend the cocoa powder with the warm water and add to the butter or margarine. Remove from the heat and beat in the icing sugar. Leave to cool slightly and when thick spoon over the top of the cake. Make a swirled effect with a fork and decorate with the walnut halves while the icing is still soft.

Dundee cake

Metric	Imperial
150 g butter	*6 oz butter*
150 g soft brown sugar	*6 oz soft brown sugar*
3 standard eggs, lightly beaten	*3 large eggs, lightly beaten*
150 g plain flour	*6 oz plain flour*
25 g ground almonds	*1 oz ground almonds*
1 × 5 ml spoon baking powder	*1 teaspoon baking powder*
200 g sultanas	*8 oz sultanas*
200 g currants	*8 oz currants*
75 g chopped mixed peel	*3 oz chopped mixed peel*
75 g glacé cherries, halved	*3 oz glacé cherries, halved*
1 × 5 ml spoon finely grated lemon rind	*1 teaspoon finely grated lemon rind*
1½ × 15 ml spoons lemon juice	*1½ tablespoons lemon juice*
About 20 split blanched almonds	*About 20 split blanched almonds*

Cooking Time: 2½ hours
Oven: 180°C, 350°F, Gas Mark 4;
     150°C, 300°F, Gas Mark 2

Well grease an 18 cm (7 in) cake tin and line the base and sides with greased greaseproof paper. Cream the butter and sugar until light and fluffy. Gradually beat in the eggs, adding a tablespoon of the flour with the last amount. Fold in the almonds. Sieve in the remaining flour and baking powder and fold into the creamed mixture with the dried fruit, peel, cherries, lemon rind and juice. Turn into the prepared tin and level off. Arrange the almonds on the top of the cake and brush with a little egg white; you can get enough for this by brushing inside the egg shells.

Bake in a moderate oven for 1 hour, then reduce the temperature to cool and bake for a further 1½ hours or until a skewer inserted in the centre comes out clean. Leave in the tin for 10 minutes, then carefully turn out on to a wire rack to cool.

Dundee cake

Country fruit cake; Rock cakes

Country fruit cake

Metric	Imperial
200 g self-raising flour	8 oz self-raising flour
Pinch of salt	Pinch of salt
½ teaspoon ground mixed spice	½ teaspoon ground mixed spice
75 g margarine	3 oz margarine
100 g soft brown sugar	4 oz soft brown sugar
100 g raisins	4 oz raisins
100 g sultanas	4 oz sultanas
50 g chopped mixed peel	2 oz chopped mixed peel
50 g glacé cherries, chopped	2 oz glacé cherries, chopped
1 standard egg, lightly beaten	1 large egg, lightly beaten
About 125 ml milk	About ¼ pint milk

Cooking Time: 1 hour   Oven: 190°C, 375°F, Gas Mark 5

Well grease an 18cm (7 in) cake tin and line the base with greased greaseproof paper. Sieve together the flour, salt and spice. Rub in the margarine. Add the sugar, raisins, sultanas, peel and cherries. Add the egg and sufficient milk so that the mixture will drop from a spoon when shaken. Turn into the prepared tin. Bake in a moderately hot oven for 1 hour or until the cake is golden and a skewer inserted into the centre comes out clean. Leave in the tin for 5 minutes, turn out on to a wire rack and cool.

Rock cakes

Metric	Imperial
200 g self-raising flour	8 oz self-raising flour
½ teaspoon salt	½ teaspoon salt
Pinch of mixed spice	Pinch of mixed spice
75 g margarine	3 oz margarine
75 g caster sugar	3 oz caster sugar
75 g mixed dried fruit	3 oz mixed dried fruit
1 standard egg, lightly beaten	1 large egg, lightly beaten
1½ × 15 ml spoons milk	2 tablespoons milk
Demerara sugar	Demerara sugar

Cooking Time: 10–15 minutes
Oven: 200°C, 400°F, Gas Mark 6

Sieve together the flour, salt and mixed spice. Rub in the margarine until the mixture resembles fine breadcrumbs. Add the sugar and fruit. Mix the egg and milk together and pour into the ingredients. Mix well with a fork to a stiff, rough dough.
Put 12 spoonfuls of the mixture on a greased baking tray, rough up with a fork and sprinkle each cake with a little demerara sugar. Bake in a moderately hot oven for 10–15 minutes or until golden brown.
Makes 12

Rich fruit cake

Metric	Imperial
225 g plain flour	*9 oz plain flour*
¼ teaspoon salt	*¼ teaspoon salt*
1 × 5 ml spoon ground mixed spice	*1 teaspoon ground mixed spice*
200 g butter	*8 oz butter*
200 g dark brown sugar	*8 oz dark brown sugar*
2 × 15 ml spoons black treacle	*2 tablespoons black treacle*
½ teaspoon vanilla essence	*½ teaspoon vanilla essence*
4 standard eggs, lightly beaten	*4 large eggs, lightly beaten*
800 g mixed dried fruit	*2 lb mixed dried fruit*
100 g chopped mixed peel	*4 oz chopped mixed peel*
150 g glacé cherries, halved	*6 oz glacé cherries, halved*
100 g blanched almonds chopped	*4 oz blanched almonds, chopped*
3 × 15 ml spoons brandy	*3 tablespoons brandy*

Cooking Time: 3–4 hours
Oven: 150°C, 300°F, Gas Mark 2

Grease a 20 cm (8 in) round or an 18 cm (7 in) square cake tin and line the base and sides with a double layer of greased greaseproof paper. A band of brown paper tied round the outside of the tin will help prevent it from becoming too browned while cooking.

Sieve together the flour, salt and mixed spice. Cream the butter, sugar, treacle and vanilla essence together until light and fluffy. Beat in the eggs, a little at a time, adding a tablespoon of the flour with the last amount. Fold in the remaining flour, then all the fruit and almonds. Turn into the prepared cake tin and make a slight hollow in the centre. Bake in a cool oven for 3–4 hours, testing after three hours by inserting a skewer into the centre; when it comes out clean the cake is cooked. Remove from the oven and leave in the tin for at least 15 minutes. Turn out on to a wire rack and leave to cool. Make a few holes in the top of the cake with a skewer and pour over the brandy. Wrap the cake in greaseproof paper and store in an airtight tin for at least a week before using.

Christmas cake

Metric	Imperial
1 × 18–20 cm baked rich fruit cake, see above	*1 × 7–8 in baked rich fruit cake, see above*
For the almond paste:	**For the almond paste:**
300 g ground almonds	*12 oz ground almonds*
150 g icing sugar, sieved	*6 oz icing sugar, sieved*
150 g caster sugar	*6 oz caster sugar*
4 standard egg yolks	*4 large egg yolks*
3 × 15 ml spoons lemon juice	*3 tablespoons lemon juice*
Apricot jam, sieved	*Apricot jam, sieved*
For the royal icing:	**For the royal icing:**
3 standard egg whites	*3 large egg whites*
600 g icing sugar, sieved	*1½ lb icing sugar, sieved*
1½ × 5 ml spoons liquid glycerine (optional)	*1½ teaspoons liquid glycerine (optional)*
1 × 15 ml spoon lemon juice	*1 tablespoon lemon juice*

Mix the ground almonds with the sugars. Add the egg yolks and lemon juice and mix to a pliable paste. Place on a working surface or board lightly dusted with icing sugar and knead until smooth and free from cracks. Brush the top and sides of the cake with sieved apricot jam. Roll out just over half the almond paste and cut into a circle the same size as the cake. Place on the top of the cake. Roll out the remaining paste and cut into two strips, each the depth and half the circumference of the cake. Place these round the sides of the cake. Put the cake into a cool place and leave for at least 1 day or up to 3 days for the paste to harden before icing. Stand the cake on a cake board to ice. Lightly whisk the egg whites, then add the sugar a little at a time, beating well between each addition, until the icing is smooth and stiff enough to form peaks. Add the glycerine and lemon juice; the glycerine is not essential but stops the icing from becoming too brittle. Spread the icing all over the top and sides of the cake, swirling it up with a round bladed knife to give a rough finish. Decorate with washed holly and Christmas ornaments while the icing is still soft. Leave to set.

Orange tutti-frutti cake

Orange tutti-frutti cake

Metric	Imperial
100 g butter	4 oz butter
100 g caster sugar	4 oz caster sugar
2 × 5 ml spoons finely grated orange rind	2 teaspoons finely grated orange rind
2 standard eggs, lightly beaten	2 large eggs, lightly beaten
75 g self-raising flour	3 oz self-raising flour
50 g fresh white breadcrumbs	2 oz fresh white breadcrumbs
50 g prunes, stoned and finely chopped	2 oz prunes, stoned and finely chopped
50 g glacé cherries, finely chopped	2 oz glacé cherries, finely chopped
50 g dried apricots, finely chopped	2 oz apricots, finely chopped
25 g chopped mixed peel	1 oz chopped mixed peel

For the icing:
75 g butter
150 g icing sugar, sieved
1 × 15 ml spoon orange juice

For the icing:
3 oz butter
6 oz icing sugar, sieved
1 tablespoon orange juice

To decorate:
½ orange

To decorate:
½ orange

Cooking Time: 1 hour   Oven: 180°C, 350°F, Gas Mark 4

Well grease an 18 cm (7 in) cake tin and line the base with greased greaseproof paper. Cream the butter, sugar and orange rind until light and fluffy. Gradually beat in the eggs, adding a tablespoon of the flour with the last amount. Sieve in the flour and fold into the creamed mixture. Fold in the breadcrumbs, then the chopped fruit. Turn the mixture into the prepared tin and level off. Bake in a moderate oven for 1 hour or until golden brown. Leave in the tin for 5 minutes, then turn out on to a wire rack.

Beat the butter, then beat in the icing sugar and orange juice. Spread all over the top and sides of the cake. Peel the half orange, removing all the white pith. Slice across in rings and cut each ring in half. Use to decorate the cake.

Easy no-flour fruit cake; Boiled fruit cake

Boiled fruit cake

Metric	Imperial
150 g mixed dried fruit	6 oz mixed dried fruit
75 g margarine	3 oz margarine
75 g soft brown sugar	3 oz soft brown sugar
1 × 5 ml spoon ground mixed spice	1 teaspoon ground mixed spice
200 ml water	7½ fl oz water
200 g plain flour	8 oz plain flour
1 × 5 ml spoon bicarbonate of soda	1 teaspoon bicarbonate of of soda
½ teaspoon salt	½ teaspoon salt

Cooking Time: 1½ hours   Oven: 180°C, 350°F, Gas Mark 4

Grease a 15 cm (6 in) cake tin and line the base and sides with greased greaseproof paper. Put the fruit, margarine, sugar, spice and water in a pan. Bring to the boil and boil for 3 minutes. Allow to cool. Sieve the flour, bicarbonate of soda and salt and pour in the boiled mixture. Beat well and turn into the prepared tin. Bake in a moderate oven for 1½ hours or until a skewer inserted into the centre comes out clean. Leave in the tin for 5 minutes, then turn out on to a wire rack to cool.

Easy no-flour fruit cake

Metric	Imperial
400 g mincemeat	1 lb mincemeat
400 g mixed dried fruit	1 lb mixed dried fruit
100 g glacé cherries, halved	4 oz glacé cherries, halved
100 g walnuts, chopped	4 oz walnuts, chopped
200 g cornflakes, crushed	8 oz cornflakes, crushed
3 standard eggs, lightly beaten	3 large eggs, lightly beaten
1 large can condensed milk (equivalent to about 1.125 l of skimmed milk)	1 large can condensed milk (equivalent to 1⅞ pints of skimmed milk)
1 × 5 ml spoon mixed spice	1 teaspoon mixed spice
1 × 5 ml spoon baking powder	1 teaspoon baking powder

Cooking Time: 1¼ hours   Oven: 150°C, 300°F, Gas Mark 2

Grease a 25 cm (10 in) round cake tin and line the base with greased greaseproof paper. Put all the ingredients into a mixing bowl and blend well. Turn into the prepared cake tin and level off. Bake in a cool oven for 1¼ hours. Leave in the tin for 10 minutes, then turn out on to a wire rack to cool.

Greek yogurt cake

Metric	Imperial
150 g plain flour	6 oz plain flour
1 × 5 ml spoon bicarbonate of soda	1 teaspoon bicarbonate of soda
½ teaspoon salt	½ teaspoon salt
50 g butter	2 oz butter
150 g caster sugar	6 oz caster sugar
3 standard eggs, separated	3 large eggs, separated
125 ml natural yogurt	¼ pint natural yogurt
2 × 5 ml spoons finely grated lemon rind	2 teaspoons finely grated lemon rind

For the icing:	For the icing:
100 g icing sugar, sieved	4 oz icing sugar, sieved
About 1¼ × 15 ml spoons lemon juice	About 1¼ tablespoons lemon juice
Crystallised violets	Crystallised violets

Cooking Time: 1¼ hours   Oven 180°C, 350°F, Gas Mark 4

Grease a 20 cm (8 in) cake tin and line the base with greased greaseproof paper. Sieve the flour, bicarbonate of soda and salt. Cream the butter until soft. Add the sugar and egg yolks and mix thoroughly; at this stage the mixture will be very crumbly. Add the yogurt and lemon rind and beat well. Gradually stir in the sieved flour. Whisk the egg whites until they form stiff peaks, then carefully fold into the yogurt mixture. Turn into the prepared cake tin. Bake in a moderate oven for 1¼ hours. Leave in the tin for a few minutes, then turn out and cool on a wire rack.
Blend the icing sugar with enough lemon juice to give a thick, coating consistency. Carefully spoon over the top of the cake, place the crystallised violets in position and leave to set.
Note: This cake improves if kept uncut for a day.

Moist gingerbread

Metric	Imperial
100 g margarine	4 oz margarine
150 g black treacle	6 oz black treacle
50 g golden syrup	2 oz golden syrup
125 ml milk	¼ pint milk
2 standard eggs, lightly beaten	2 large eggs, lightly beaten
200 g plain flour	8 oz plain flour
50 g caster sugar	2 oz caster sugar
1 × 5 ml spoon mixed spice	1 teaspoon mixed spice
1 × 5 ml spoon bicarbonate of soda	1 teaspoon bicarbonate of soda
2 × 5 ml spoons ground ginger	2 teaspoons ground ginger

Cooking Time: 1¼–1½ hours
Oven: 170°C, 325°F, Gas Mark 3

Grease an 18–20 cm (7–8 in) square cake tin and line the base and sides with greased greaseproof paper. Put the margarine, treacle and syrup into a saucepan. Heat gently until the margarine has melted, stirring from time to time, then remove from the heat and add the milk. Allow to cool for 5 minutes, then add the beaten eggs.
Sieve the dry ingredients into a mixing bowl, then add the treacle mixture and beat well together. Pour into the prepared cake tin and cook in a very moderate oven for 1¼–1½ hours. Turn out of the tin and leave to cool on a wire rack. When the gingerbread is quite cold put into an airtight tin and leave for 2–3 days before eating, if possible.
Variations
Add 100 g (4 oz) raisins, dried fruit or chopped dates.
Replace 100 g (4 oz) of the plain flour with wholemeal.

Yorkshire parkin

Metric	Imperial
200 g plain flour	8 oz plain flour
Pinch of salt	Pinch of salt
2 × 5 ml spoons ground ginger	2 teaspoons ground ginger
½ teaspoon ground cinnamon	½ teaspoon ground cinnamon
1 × 5 ml spoon bicarbonate of soda	1 teaspoon bicarbonate of soda
200 g medium oatmeal	8 oz medium oatmeal
150 g black treacle	6 oz black treacle
150 g lard or margarine	6 oz lard or margarine
100 g soft brown sugar	4 oz soft brown sugar
1 standard egg, lightly beaten	1 large egg, lightly beaten
125 ml milk	¼ pint milk

Cooking Time: 1¼ hours   Oven: 180°C, 350°F, Gas Mark 4

Well grease a 23 cm (9 in) square cake tin and line the base and sides with greased greaseproof paper. Sieve the flour, salt, ginger, cinnamon, and bicarbonate of soda into a mixing bowl. Add the oatmeal and put on one side. Put the treacle, lard or margarine and sugar into a pan. Heat gently until the butter has melted and the sugar dissolved. Remove from the heat and pour into the flour. Add the egg and milk and beat to a smooth batter. Pour into the prepared cake tin and bake in a moderate oven for 1¼ hours. Leave in the tin for about 5 minutes then turn out and cool on a wire rack. Store in an airtight tin for a week before serving, on its own or spread with butter.

Yorkshire parkin; Iced honey gingercake; Moist gingerbread; Greek yogurt cake

Iced honey gingercake

Metric

125 g butter or margarine
100 g soft brown sugar
150 g clear honey
1 × 15 ml spoon water
175 g self-raising flour
½ teaspoon ground mixed spice
2 × 5 ml spoons ground ginger
2 standard eggs, lightly beaten

For the icing and decoration:
300 g icing sugar, sieved
About 3 × 15 ml spoons syrup from preserved ginger
Few pieces preserved ginger, sliced

Imperial

5 oz butter or margarine
4 oz soft brown sugar
6 oz clear honey
1 tablespoon water
7 oz self-raising flour
½ teaspoon ground mixed spice
2 teaspoons ground ginger
2 large eggs, lightly beaten

For the icing and decoration:
12 oz icing sugar, sieved
About 3 tablespoons syrup from preserved ginger
Few pieces preserved ginger, sliced

Cooking Time: 45 minutes
Oven: 180°C, 350°F, Gas Mark 4

Grease a 750 ml (1½ pint) ring mould. Put the butter or margarine, sugar, honey and water into a pan. Stand over a gentle heat until the fat has melted and the sugar dissolved. Remove from the heat and cool for 10 minutes. Sieve the flour, spice and ginger into a bowl. Pour in the melted fat and eggs and beat well. Turn the mixture into the prepared mould and bake in a moderate oven for about 45 minutes or until well risen and firm to the touch. Leave in the tin for 2–3 minutes, then turn out on to a wire rack and leave to cool.
Blend the icing sugar with enough preserved ginger syrup to give a flowing icing. Spoon carefully over the gingerbread, making sure it is evenly iced. Decorate the top of the cake with slices of preserved ginger.

Iced banana loaf

Metric	Imperial
200 g self-raising flour	8 oz self-raising flour
½ teaspoon salt	½ teaspoon salt
¼ teaspoon mixed spice	¼ teaspoon mixed spice
100 g butter or margarine	4 oz butter or margarine
400 g ripe bananas	1 lb ripe bananas
150 g caster sugar	6 oz caster sugar
100 g chopped mixed peel	4 oz chopped mixed peel
50 g walnuts, roughly chopped	2 oz walnuts, roughly chopped
2 standard eggs, lightly beaten	2 large eggs, lightly beaten
For the icing:	For the icing:
100 g icing sugar, sieved	4 oz icing sugar, sieved
About 1 × 15 ml spoon water	About 1 tablespoon water
Few walnut halves	Few walnut halves
Quartered slices of orange	Quartered slices of orange

Cooking Time: 1 hour 10 minutes
Oven: 180°C, 350°F, Gas Mark 4

Well grease and flour a 600 g (1½ lb) loaf tin. Sieve the flour, salt and spice into a bowl. Rub in the butter or margarine until the mixture resembles fine breadcrumbs. Peel and mash the bananas and add to the flour with the remaining ingredients. Beat until the mixture is well blended. Turn into the prepared tin and bake in a moderate oven for 1 hour 10 minutes or until the loaf is well risen and pale golden. Leave in the tin for 5 minutes and cool on a wire rack. When the loaf is quite cold, blend the icing sugar and water to give a thick, flowing icing. Spoon over the top of the loaf and decorate with a few walnut halves and quartered orange slices.

Hazelnut and honey cake

Metric	Imperial
150 g whole hazelnuts	6 oz whole hazelnuts
3 standard eggs, lightly beaten	3 large eggs, lightly beaten
125 g self-raising flour	5 oz self-raising flour
50 g caster sugar	2 oz caster sugar
50 g butter, softened	2 oz butter, softenend
100 g clear honey	4 oz clear honey

Cooking Time: 35–40 minutes
Oven: 180°C, 350°F, Gas Mark 4

Scatter the nuts on a baking tray and put into a moderate oven for 10 minutes. Allow to cool, then rub the nuts between your hands to remove the brown skins. Chop finely. Well grease and line the base of a shallow 20 cm (8 in) cake tin.
Blend the eggs, flour and sugar together in a bowl. Stir in the nuts, then the butter and honey. Turn into the prepared tin and bake in a moderate oven for 35–40 minutes or until golden brown. Leave in the tin for 5 minutes, then turn out and cool on a wire rack.

Plum bread

Metric	Imperial
1 × 5 ml spoon sugar	1 teaspoon sugar
250 ml warm milk	½ pint warm milk
2 × 5 ml spoons dried yeast	2 teaspoons dried yeast
300 g self-raising flour	12 oz self-raising flour
1 × 5 ml spoon salt	1 teaspoon salt
½ teaspoon ground mixed spice	½ teaspoon ground mixed spice
100 g butter	4 oz butter
150 g caster sugar	6 oz caster sugar
75 g sultanas	3 oz sultanas
50 g glacé cherries, quartered	2 oz glacé cherries, quartered
150 g currants	6 oz currants
75 g seedless raisins	3 oz seedless raisins
50 g chopped mixed peel	2 oz chopped mixed peel

Cooking Time: 2 hours   Oven: 150°C, 300°F, Gas Mark 2

Well grease and flour an 800 g (2 lb) loaf tin. Dissolve the sugar in the warm milk, sprinkle over the yeast and leave for about 10 minutes in a warm place until frothy. Sieve together the flour, salt and spice. Rub in the butter. Add the sugar and all the fruit.
Pour in the yeast liquid and mix to a fairly stiff dough. Place the mixture in the prepared tin and level off. Bake in a cool oven for 2 hours. Leave to cool in the tin, then turn out and keep for at least two days in an airtight tin before eating.

Iced banana loaf; Hazelnut and honey cake; Cornish saffron cake; Plum bread

Cornish saffron cake

Metric

1 × 5 ml spoon sugar
200 ml warm milk
2 × 5 ml spoons dried yeast
1 small sachet (0.5 g)
powdered saffron or few
strands saffron
125 ml boiling water
400 g plain flour
1 × 5 ml spoon salt
100 g margarine
25 g caster sugar
150 g currants
100 g chopped mixed peel

Imperial

1 teaspoon sugar
Scant ½ pint warm milk
2 teaspoons dried yeast
1 small sachet (0.5 g)
powdered saffron or few
strands saffron
¼ pint boiling water
1 lb plain flour
1 teaspoon salt
4 oz margarine
1 oz caster sugar
6 oz currants
4 oz chopped mixed peel

Cooking Time: 1 hour
Oven: 200°C, 400°F, Gas Mark 6;
      180°C, 350°F, Gas Mark 4

Thoroughly grease a 20 cm (8 in) cake tin. Dissolve the sugar in the warm milk, sprinkle over the dried yeast and leave for about 10 minutes or until frothy. Pour the boiling water over the saffron and leave to cool. Strain if using saffron strands.

Sieve the flour and salt and rub in the margarine. Add the sugar, currants and peel. Add the saffron liquid and the yeast liquid and mix to a soft dough. Turn into the prepared cake tin and cover with a damp cloth. Leave to rise until the dough comes to the top of the tin – 1 hour in a warm place or 2 hours at average room temperature. Remove the cloth and bake in a moderately hot oven for 30 minutes, then reduce the temperature and bake for a further 30 minutes. Leave in the tin for 2–3 minutes, then turn out and cool on a wire rack.

Swiss hazelnut and carrot cake

Metric	Imperial
200 g carrots	*8 oz carrots*
3 standard eggs, separated	*3 large eggs, separated*
125 g sugar	*5 oz sugar*
125 g hazelnuts, very finely chopped	*5 oz hazelnuts, very finely chopped*
2 × 5 ml spoons finely grated lemon rind	*2 teaspoons finely grated lemon rind*
50 g plain flour	*2 oz plain flour*
½ teaspoon baking powder	*½ teaspoon baking powder*

Cooking Time: 40–45 minutes
Oven: 180°C, 350°F, Gas Mark 4

Well grease an 18 cm (7 in) square tin. Peel and grate the carrots and re-weigh; you should have about 125 g (5 oz). Whisk the egg yolks and the sugar until thick and creamy. Stir in the carrots, hazelnuts and lemon rind. Sieve in the flour and baking powder and fold in. Whisk the egg whites until they form stiff peaks, then carefully fold into the mixture. Turn into the prepared cake tin and bake in a moderate oven for 40–45 minutes. Leave in the tin for 2–3 minutes, then turn out on to a wire rack to cool.

Swiss hazelnut and carrot cake

Norwegian apple cake

Metric

2 standard eggs
225 g caster sugar
100 g butter
150 ml top of the
milk or creamy milk
175 g plain flour
3 × 5 ml spoons baking
powder
3–4 Bramley cooking
apples

Imperial

2 large eggs
9 oz caster sugar
4 oz butter
Generous ¼ pint top of the
milk or creamy milk
6½ oz plain flour
3 teaspoons baking
powder
3–4 Bramley cooking
apples

Cooking Time: 20–25 minutes
Oven: 200°C, 400°F, Gas Mark 6

Grease and flour a 20 × 30 cm (8 × 12 in) roasting tin. Whisk the eggs and 200 g (8 oz) of the sugar until the mixture is thick and creamy and the whisk leaves a trail when it is lifted out. Put the butter and milk into a pan. Bring to the boil and stir, still boiling, into the eggs and sugar. Sieve in the flour and baking powder and fold carefully into the batter so that there are no lumps of flour. Pour the mixture into the prepared roasting tin. Peel, core and slice the apples; arrange them over the batter. Sprinkle with the remaining sugar. Bake in a moderately hot oven for 20–25 minutes until well risen and golden brown. Cool in the tin, then cut into slices.

Norwegian apple cake

Spicy nut and date cake

Metric	Imperial
300 g plain flour	12 oz plain flour
Pinch of salt	Pinch of salt
2 × 5 ml spoons ground cinnamon	2 teaspoons ground cinnamon
150 g margarine	6 oz margarine
150 g caster sugar	6 oz caster sugar
150 g chopped mixed nuts	6 oz chopped mixed nuts
150 g stoned dates, chopped	6 oz stoned dates, chopped
410 g can apple purée	14½ oz can apple purée
1½ × 5 ml spoons bicarbonate of soda	1½ teaspoons bicarbonate of soda
2 × 5 ml spoons milk	1 tablespoon milk

Cooking Time: 1¼–1½ hours
Oven: 180°C, 350°F, Gas Mark 4

Grease a 23 cm (9 in) round cake tin and line the base with greased greaseproof paper. Sieve together the flour, salt and cinnamon. Rub in the margarine until the mixture resembles fine breadcrumbs. Add the sugar, nuts and dates. Make a well in the centre of the mixture and add the apple purée. Dissolve the bicarbonate of soda in the milk and add to the mixture. Beat well. Turn into the prepared tin and bake in a moderate oven for 1¼–1½ hours. Leave in the tin for 5 minutes, then turn out and cool on a wire rack.

Swedish cardamom cake

Metric	Imperial
100 g butter	4 oz butter
200 g caster sugar	8 oz caster sugar
2 × 5 ml spoons ground cardamom	2 teaspoons ground cardamom
1 standard egg, beaten	1 large egg, beaten
125 ml single cream	¼ pint single cream
300 g self-raising flour	12 oz self-raising flour
For the icing:	For the icing:
About 1 × 15 ml spoon lemon juice	About 1 tablespoon lemon juice
100 g icing sugar, sieved	4 oz icing sugar, sieved
Lemon rind, thinly peeled	Lemon rind, thinly peeled

Cooking Time: 40–45 minutes
Oven: 180°C, 350°F, Gas Mark 4

Well grease a 23 cm (9 in) ring mould and dust with flour. Melt the butter and pour over the sugar in a bowl. Beat in the cardamom, egg and cream, then stir in the sieved flour. Turn into the prepared tin and level off. Bake in a moderate oven for 40–45 minutes or until well risen and pale golden. Leave in the tin for 2 minutes, then turn out on to a wire rack to cool.

When the cake is cold blend the lemon juice into the icing sugar to a thick, flowing icing. Spoon over the top of the cake, allowing it to run down the sides. Cut the lemon peel into long strips. Put into a basin, cover with boiling water and leave for 5 minutes, then drain and dry well. Decorate the top of the cake with these strips.

American brownies

Metric	Imperial
2 standard eggs	2 large eggs
200 g caster sugar	8 oz caster sugar
50 g butter, melted	2 oz butter, melted
½ teaspoon vanilla essence	½ teaspoon vanilla essence
50 g plain flour	2 oz plain flour
3 × 15 ml spoons cocoa powder	3 tablespoons cocoa powder
½ teaspoon baking powder	½ teaspoon baking powder
Pinch of salt	Pinch of salt
50 g walnuts, roughly chopped	2 oz walnuts, roughly chopped

Cooking Time: 30 minutes
Oven: 190°C, 375°F, Gas Mark 5

Well grease a 20 cm (8 in) square tin. Whisk the eggs and sugar together until the mixture is thick and creamy. Beat in the butter and vanilla essence. Sieve in the flour, cocoa, baking powder and salt and fold into the mixture with the walnuts. Turn into the prepared tin and bake in a moderately hot oven for 30 minutes. Leave in the tin for 10 minutes, then cut the brownies into squares and remove while still warm.

Spicy nut and date cake; American brownies; Swedish cardamom cake; Treacle and walnut streusel loaf

Treacle and walnut streusel loaf

Metric

For filling and topping:
100 g demerara sugar
25 g butter, melted
100 g walnuts, chopped
*1 × 5 ml spoon ground
cinnamon*

For the loaf:
100 g black treacle
125 ml milk
2 standard eggs, beaten
250 g self-raising flour
50 g butter
100 g stoned dates, chopped

Imperial

For filling and topping:
4 oz demerara sugar
1 oz butter, melted
4 oz walnuts, chopped
*1 teaspoon ground
cinnamon*

For the loaf:
4 oz black treacle
¼ pint milk
2 large eggs, beaten
10 oz self-raising flour
2 oz butter
4 oz stoned dates, chopped

Cooking Time: 1 hour   Oven: 180°C, 350°F, Gas Mark 4

Well grease an 800 g (2 lb) loaf tin. Mix all the ingredients for the filling and topping together. Blend together the treacle, milk and beaten eggs. Sieve the flour into a bowl and rub in the butter. Add the dates. Make a well in the centre and pour in the treacle mixture. Blend well. Turn half the mixture into the prepared tin and sprinkle with half the walnut mixture. Cover with the remaining cake mixture and top with the last of the walnut mixture. Bake in a moderate oven for 1 hour. Leave in the tin for 5 minutes, then turn out and cool on a wire rack.

The gâteaux in this chapter can either be served for tea or coffee, or they will make delicious desserts which can, of course, be prepared well in advance. Many of them are from Denmark, Germany, Austria and Hungary, countries renowned for their patisserie.

Children's birthday cakes are always very important to them and two ideas are given here for novelty cakes – a racing track cake and an engine. These two are slightly complicated, but just using two baked 18 cm (7 in) Victoria sandwiches (page 9) you can make all sorts of different cakes. Sandwich the cakes together and cover the sides with red butter icing and the top with yellow butter icing for a circus ring and put animals and circus men in the centre. Or simply sandwich the cakes together and ice the top with a thick glacé icing or butter icing, then cut out numbers and clock hands in coloured marzipan and place in position on top of the cake.

Little girls in particular will love a maypole. Sandwich the cakes together and ice the top with a thick glacé icing. Cover a stick or piece of dowelling with different coloured ribbons and place in the centre of the cake. Tie on as many different coloured streamers to the pole as there are children for the party, and tie a small bunch of fresh flowers with their name on to each of the streamers.

The Christmas house on page 48 is a traditional feature of a German family Christmas. You can make it a week or so before Christmas and just keep it in a cool place.

Danish layer cake

Metric	*Imperial*
4 standard eggs, separated	4 large eggs, separated
1 × 5 ml spoon finely grated lemon rind	1 teaspoon finely grated lemon rind
2 × 15 ml spoons lemon juice	2 tablespoons lemon juice
125 g icing sugar, sieved	5 oz icing sugar, sieved
75 g plain flour	3 oz plain flour
25 g cornflour	1 oz cornflour
½ teaspoon baking powder	½ teaspoon baking powder

For the filling:

Metric	*Imperial*
2 × 5 ml spoons powdered gelatine	2 teaspoons powdered gelatine
2 × 15 ml spoons cold water	2 tablespoons cold water
500 ml double cream	1 pint double cream
2 × 15 ml spoons caster sugar	2 tablespoons caster sugar
2 × 15 ml spoons kirsch (optional)	2 tablespoons kirsch (optional)
396 g can pineapple pieces, drained and chopped	14 oz can pineapple pieces, drained and chopped
75 g bitter or plain chocolate, grated	3 oz bitter or plain chocolate, grated

Cooking Time: 35–40 minutes
Oven: 180°C, 350°F, Gas Mark 4

Grease a 20 cm (8 in) cake tin and line the base with greased greaseproof paper. Whisk the egg yolks, lemon rind and juice and sugar together until pale and creamy, and the mixture falls from the whisk in a smooth ribbon. Whisk the egg whites until they form stiff peaks. Sieve the flour, cornflour and baking powder together and gently fold into the egg yolks, one-third at a time with the egg whites. Turn into the prepared tin and bake in a moderate oven for 35–40 minutes. Leave in the tin for 5 minutes, then turn out and cool on a wire rack. When cold, cut the cake into three rounds.

Sprinkle the gelatine over the cold water in a basin and leave to soften for 5 minutes. Stand the basin over a pan of boiling water and leave until the gelatine has dissolved. Remove from the heat and allow to cool slightly. Lightly whip two-thirds of the cream and beat in the gelatine, sugar and kirsch, if using. Fold in the pineapple and chocolate. Put the filling on one side and leave until set.

Spread each layer of sponge evenly with the filling and reassemble the cake. Whip the remaining cream and pipe on top of the cake to decorate. Chill for about 1 hour before serving.

Danish layer cake

Sachertorte

Metric	Imperial
200 g plain cooking chocolate	8 oz plain cooking chocolate
1 × 15 ml spoon strong black coffee	1 tablespoon strong black coffee
200 g butter	8 oz butter
200 g sugar	8 oz sugar
5 standard eggs, separated	5 large eggs, separated
150 g self-raising flour	6 oz self-raising flour

For the filling:

Metric	Imperial
4 × 15 ml spoons apricot jam, sieved	4 tablespoons apricot jam, sieved

For the frosting:

Metric	Imperial
150 g plain cooking chocolate	6 oz plain cooking chocolate
4 × 15 ml spoons black coffee	4 tablespoons black coffee
150 g icing sugar, sieved	6 oz icing sugar, sieved

Cooking Time: 1½ hours   Oven: 150°C, 300°F, Gas Mark 2

Grease a 23 cm (9 in) cake tin and line the base and the sides with greased greaseproof paper. Break the chocolate into small pieces and put into a basin with the coffee. Stand the basin over a pan of hot water and leave until the chocolate has melted. Allow to cool. Cream the butter and sugar until light and fluffy. Beat in the egg yolks, one at a time, then the cooled chocolate. Sieve in the flour and fold in. Whisk the egg whites until they form stiff peaks and fold into the mixture. Turn into the prepared tin and bake in a cool oven for 1½ hours. Leave the cake in the tin for 15 minutes, then turn out and cool on a wire rack. When the cake is cold split it in half, spread the bottom round with most of the apricot jam and sandwich the cake together again. Brush the remaining apricot jam all over the top and sides of the cake.

Put the chocolate, broken into pieces, and coffee into a basin over a pan of hot water. Leave until the chocolate has melted, then beat in the icing sugar. Pour the frosting over the cake and spread it evenly over the top and sides using a palette knife which has been dipped in warm water. Allow to set for at least 1 hour. Traditionally Sachertorte is always served with whipped cream.

Gâteau Diane

For the meringue:

Metric	Imperial
4 standard egg whites	4 large egg whites
200 g caster sugar	8 oz caster sugar

For the icing and filling:

Metric	Imperial
150 g plain chocolate	6 oz plain chocolate
200 g unsalted butter	8 oz unsalted butter
4 standard egg yolks	4 large egg yolks
100 g loaf or granulated sugar	4 oz loaf or granulated sugar
125 ml water	¼ pint water
396 g can pineapple, drained	14 oz can pineapple, drained

To decorate:

Metric	Imperial
75–100 g browned flaked almonds	3–4 oz browned flaked almonds

Cooking Time: 6 hours   Oven: 110°C, 225°F, Gas Mark ¼

Mark out 2 × 20 cm (8 in) circles on greased greaseproof paper or non-stick silicone paper and place on greased baking sheets. Whisk the egg whites stiffly until they form very stiff peaks. Whisk in the sugar, a teaspoon at a time if using an electric whisk. If whisking by hand add half the sugar a teaspoon at a time and fold in the remainder. Divide the meringue mixture between the two circles and spread it out so that it is very even and comes right to the edges. Bake in a very slow oven for about 6 hours, or overnight, until the meringue is hard. Remove from oven and cool.

Melt the chocolate in a basin over a pan of hot water. Cream the butter and beat in the chocolate. Lightly beat the egg yolks in a separate basin. Put the sugar with the water into a saucepan over a gentle heat until the sugar has dissolved, then boil rapidly to 110°C (225°F) or until the syrup forms a long thread when dropped in a bowl of cold water. Beat gradually into the egg yolks, and whisk to a mousse-like consistency, then add this slowly to the butter mixture. Spread a layer of chocolate icing and half the pineapple, roughly chopped, on one round of meringue. Place the second meringue on top. Cover the sides of the meringues with most of the remaining chocolate icing and roll in the flaked browned almonds. Spread the last of the icing over the top and decorate with the remaining pineapple.

Sachertorte; Star cake; Gâteau Diane

Star cake

Metric	Imperial
50 g unsalted butter	*2 oz unsalted butter*
75 g plain flour	*3 oz plain flour*
4 standard eggs	*4 large eggs*
100 g caster sugar	*4 oz caster sugar*

For the filling and decoration:
250 ml double cream, lightly whipped
200 g fresh fruit – raspberries, strawberries, blackberries or currants
Sugar to taste

For the filling and decoration:
½ pint double cream, lightly whipped
8 oz fresh fruit – raspberries, strawberries, blackberries or currants
Sugar to taste

Cooking Time: 15 minutes
Oven: 200°C, 400°F, Gas Mark 6

Grease 2 × 18 cm (7 in) sandwich tins and line the bases with greased greaseproof paper. Melt the butter in a pan and allow to cool. Sieve the flour. Whisk the eggs and sugar together until they are thick and creamy and the whisk leaves a trail when lifted out. If doing this by hand, put the bowl over a pan of gently-simmering water; this is not essential if whisking with an electric mixer. Carefully fold in half the flour, then very carefully fold in the butter, then the remaining flour. Divide the cake mixture between the two tins. Level off the mixture and bake in a moderately hot oven for 15 minutes or until the cakes are golden brown and spring back when lightly pressed. Leave in the tins for 2–3 minutes, turn out and cool on a wire rack. Cut out a 10 cm (4 in) circle from the centre of one of the sponges. Spread most of the cream on to the other sponge and place the cut-out sponge on top. Pile the fruit, sprinkled with a little sugar, into the centre of the cake, reserving 6 for decoration. Cut the sponge centre in half and then into 6 wedges. Arrange round the edge of the sponge with the points facing outwards. Pile or pipe a spoonful of cream between each one and top with the reserved fruit.

39

Black forest gâteau

Metric	Imperial
100 g puff pastry (page 80) or use a 212 g packet frozen puff pastry, thawed	*4 oz puff pastry (page 80) or use a 7½ oz packet frozen puff pastry, thawed*
3 standard eggs	*3 large eggs*
75 g caster sugar	*3 oz caster sugar*
¼ teaspoon vanilla essence	*¼ teaspoon vanilla essence*
65 g self-raising flour	*2½ oz self-raising flour*
1 × 15 ml spoon cocoa powder	*1 tablespoon cocoa powder*
1 × 15 ml spoon hot water	*1 tablespoon hot water*

For the filling and decoration:	For the filling and decoration:
4 × 15 ml spoons kirsch	*4 tablespoons kirsch*
50 g caster sugar	*2 oz caster sugar*
250 ml double cream, lightly whipped	*½ pint double cream, lightly whipped*
396 g can black cherries, drained	*14 oz can black cherries, drained*
50 g plain chocolate	*2 oz plain chocolate*

Cooking Time: 30 minutes
Oven: 230°C, 450°F, Gas Mark 8;
      190°C, 375°F, Gas Mark 5

Roll out the pastry and cut out a 22 cm (8½ in) circle. Place on a damp baking sheet and bake in a very hot oven for about 12 minutes or until golden brown. Remove from the oven and cool on the tin.

Grease 2 × 20 cm (8 in) sandwich tins and line the bases with greased greaseproof paper. Whisk the eggs, sugar and the vanilla essence together until thick and creamy and the whisk leaves a trail when lifted out. Sieve in the flour and cocoa, then fold into the mixture. Lastly fold in the hot water. Divide the mixture between the two tins. Level off and bake in a moderately hot oven for about 15 minutes or until the cakes spring back when lightly pressed. Cool in the tins for 2–3 minutes then turn out on to a wire rack. Fold the kirsch and sugar into the cream. Spread the puff pastry with about a quarter of the cream, then cover with half the cherries. Put one of the cakes on top and trim the edges of the puff pastry to the same size. Spread the cake with another quarter of the cream and the remaining cherries. Top with the second cake and place on a serving plate. Spread the remaining cream over the top and sides. Melt the chocolate in a basin over a pan of hot water. Spread on to a cool surface, such as marble or Formica, and leave to set. Draw a sharp knife over the surface, pushing it away from you, to form long curls. Arrange these on top of the gâteau.

Strawberry layer gâteau

Metric	Imperial
200 g butter	*8 oz butter*
200 g caster sugar	*8 oz caster sugar*
4 standard eggs, beaten	*4 large eggs, beaten*
50 g ground almonds	*2 oz ground almonds*
150 g self-raising flour	*6 oz self-raising flour*

For the filling and decoration:	For the filling and decoration:
400 g strawberries	*1 lb strawberries*
250 ml double cream, lightly whipped	*½ pint double cream, lightly whipped*

Cooking Time: 25–30 minutes
Oven: 180°C, 350°F, Gas Mark 4

Grease 2 × 22–23 cm (8½–9 in) sandwich tins and line the bases with greased greaseproof paper. Cream the butter and sugar until light and fluffy. Gradually beat in the eggs, adding a tablespoon of the almonds with the last amount. Sieve in the flour and fold into the mixture with the remaining almonds. Turn into the prepared tins and bake in a moderate oven for 25–30 minutes or until the cakes are golden brown. Leave in the tins for 2–3 minutes, then turn out on to a wire rack and allow to cool. These layers will keep well in a tin for 2–3 days before filling and decorating.

Halve the strawberries, or quarter if they are very large. Spread one-third of the cream and half the strawberries on one of the sponges. Sandwich the cakes together and spread half the remaining cream on the top sponge. Use the remainder of the cream to pipe rosettes all round the edge. Decorate the top with the remaining strawberries.

Raspberry ice-cream cake; Raisin cheesecake; Coffee-soaked gâteau

Coffee-soaked gâteau

Metric	Imperial
150 g butter	*6 oz butter*
150 g caster sugar	*6 oz caster sugar*
3 standard eggs, lightly beaten	*3 large eggs, lightly beaten*
150 g self-raising flour	*6 oz self-raising flour*

For the coffee syrup:	For the coffee syrup:
200 g sugar	*8 oz sugar*
375 ml water	*¾ pint water*
3 × 15 ml spoons strong black coffee	*3 tablespoons strong black coffee*
3 × 15 ml spoons rum	*3 tablespoons rum*

To decorate:	To decorate:
250 ml double cream, lightly whipped	*½ pint double cream, lightly whipped*
Walnut halves	*Walnut halves*

Cooking Time: 45–50 minutes
Oven: 190°C, 375°F, Gas Mark 5

Well grease a 20 cm (8 in) cake tin and line the base with greased greaseproof paper. Cream the butter and sugar until light and fluffy. Gradually beat in the eggs, adding a tablespoon of the flour with the last amount. Sieve in the flour, then fold in carefully. Turn the mixture into the prepared tin and level off. Bake in a moderately hot oven for 45–50 minutes or until the cake is golden brown and springs back when lightly pressed. Allow to cool in the tin for 5 minutes.

While the cake is cooking dissolve the sugar in the water and coffee in a pan over a low heat and add the rum.

Turn the cake out of the tin on to a serving plate. Pierce it all over with a skewer, then pour over some of the warm coffee syrup. Leave this to soak in, then pour over some more and continue to do this until the cake has absorbed all the syrup. Leave the cake to stand for at least 6 hours.

Spread the whipped cream all over the top and sides of the cake and decorate the top with walnut halves.

Raspberry ice-cream cake

Metric	Imperial
3 standard eggs, separated	*3 large eggs, separated*
4 × 15 ml spoons hot water	*4 tablespoons hot water*
150 g caster sugar	*6 oz caster sugar*
¼ teaspoon vanilla essence	*¼ teaspoon vanilla essence*
2 × 5 ml spoons finely grated lemon rind	*2 teaspoons finely grated lemon rind*
150 g plain flour	*6 oz plain flour*
50 g cornflour	*2 oz cornflour*
3 × 5 ml spoons baking powder	*3 teaspoons baking powder*

For the filling and topping:
1 litre dairy ice-cream
200 g fresh raspberries
Icing sugar, sieved

For the filling and topping:
2 pints dairy ice-cream
8 oz fresh raspberries
Icing sugar, sieved

Cooking Time: 25 minutes
Oven: 200°C, 400°F, Gas Mark 6

Well grease a 23 cm (9 in) cake tin and line the base with greased greaseproof paper. Whisk the egg yolks with the water, sugar, vanilla essence and lemon rind until the mixture is thick and creamy. Sieve together the flour, cornflour and baking powder. Whisk the egg whites until they stand in stiff peaks. Fold the flours into the egg yolk mixture, then the egg whites. Turn into the prepared tin and bake in a moderately hot oven for 25 minutes or until well risen and golden brown. Leave in the tin for 5 minutes then turn out and cool on a wire rack.
Just before serving split the cake in half. Put spoonfuls of ice-cream on the bottom layer and top with the raspberries. Replace the top layer of the cake and sprinkle with icing sugar. Serve as soon as possible.

Raisin cheesecake

Metric	Imperial
100 g shortcrust pastry (page 75)	*4 oz shortcrust pastry (page 75)*
300 g cream cheese	*12 oz cream cheese*
2 standard eggs, separated	*2 large eggs, separated*
100 g caster sugar	*4 oz caster sugar*
3 × 15 ml spoons milk	*4 tablespoons milk*
50 g plain flour	*2 oz plain flour*
½ teaspoon vanilla essence	*½ teaspoon vanilla essence*
1 × 5 ml spoon finely grated lemon rind	*1 teaspoon finely grated lemon rind*
50 g stoned or seedless raisins	*2 oz stoned or seedless raisins*

Cooking Time: 1 hour   Oven: 180°C, 350°F, Gas Mark 4

Well grease a 23 cm (9 in) loose-bottomed cake tin or spring-form pan. Roll the pastry out thinly, cut into a 23 cm (9 in) circle and place in the bottom of the tin. Beat the cream cheese, then beat in the egg yolks, sugar, milk, flour, vanilla essence, lemon rind and raisins. Mix well. Whisk the egg whites until they form stiff peaks, then fold into the cheese mixture. Turn into the tin on top of the pastry. Bake in a moderate oven for 1 hour or until the cheesecake is set. Turn off the oven and leave the cake inside to cool, for about 2 hours; this helps to prevent it from sinking in the centre. Remove from the tin before serving.

Austrian orange cake

Metric	Imperial
5 standard egg yolks	5 large egg yolks
100 g caster sugar	4 oz caster sugar
2 × 5 ml spoons finely grated orange rind	2 teaspoons finely grated orange rind
4 × 15 ml spoons orange juice	4 tablespoons orange juice
50 g fresh white breadcrumbs	2 oz fresh white breadcrumbs
125 g ground almonds	5 oz ground almonds
3 standard egg whites	3 large egg whites

For the filling and topping:	For the filling and topping:
50 g caster sugar	2 oz caster sugar
125 ml milk	¼ pint milk
2 standard egg yolks	2 large egg yolks
150 g unsalted butter	6 oz unsalted butter
2 × 5 ml spoons very finely grated orange rind	2 teaspoons very finely grated orange rind
50 g icing sugar, sieved	2 oz icing sugar, sieved
About 15 split blanched almonds	About 15 split blanched almonds
1 thin slice of orange	1 thin slice of orange

Cooking Time: 45 minutes
Oven: 180°C, 350°F, Gas Mark 4

Well grease a 23 cm (9 in) cake tin and line the base with greased greaseproof paper. Whisk the egg yolks, sugar and orange rind until thick and creamy, then gradually whisk in the fruit juice. Fold in the breadcrumbs and almonds. Stiffly whisk the egg whites and fold into the mixture. Turn into the prepared tin and bake in a moderate oven for 45 minutes until risen and pale golden. Leave in the tin for 5 minutes, then turn out on to a wire rack and leave to cool.

Put the sugar and the milk into a pan and bring to blood heat (lukewarm). Blend the egg yolks in a basin and pour in the hot milk. Beat well. Return the mixture to the top of a double saucepan or a basin over a pan of hot water and cook, stirring, until the custard thickens. Do not allow to boil or it will curdle. Pour into a small basin and cover with a circle of damp greaseproof paper to stop a skin forming. Allow to cool.

Cream the butter and orange rind until fluffy, then very gradually beat in the custard and icing sugar.

Cut the cake in half carefully, using a very sharp knife as it is so soft it breaks easily. Spread with one-third of the icing, then sandwich together. Spread half the remaining icing over the top of the cake and put the remainder into a piping bag fitted with a 1.5 cm (½ in) rose nozzle. Pipe swirls of icing round the edge and place an almond in each. Place a twist of orange in the centre.

Chocolate and rum dessert cake

Metric	Imperial
75 g self-raising flour	3 oz self-raising flour
25 g cocoa powder	1 oz cocoa powder
4 standard eggs	4 large eggs
100 g caster sugar	4 oz caster sugar
3 × 15 ml spoons corn oil	3 tablespoons corn oil

For the butter cream:	For the butter cream:
125 g butter	5 oz butter
200 g icing sugar, sieved	8 oz icing sugar, sieved
3 × 15 ml spoons rum	3 tablespoons rum

For the icing:	For the icing:
6 × 15 ml spoons evaporated milk	6 tablespoons evaporated milk
1 × 15 ml spoon rum	1 tablespoon rum
150 g plain chocolate	6 oz plain chocolate

To decorate:	To decorate:
Crystallised ginger	Crystallised ginger

Cooking Time: about 45 minutes
Oven: 180°C, 350°F, Gas Mark 4

Grease a 20 cm (8 in) cake tin and line the base with greased greaseproof paper. Sieve together the flour and cocoa. Whisk the eggs and sugar until the mixture is thick and creamy and the whisk leaves a trail when it is lifted out. Fold in the flour then the corn oil. Turn the mixture into the prepared tin and bake in a moderate oven for about 45 minutes until the cake springs back when lightly pressed. Leave in the tin for about 3 minutes, then turn out and cool on a wire rack. Split the cake into 4 rounds.

Cream the butter, then beat in the icing sugar and the rum; do not let the butter become oily or the rum will curdle the mixture. Spread the three bottom rounds of the cakes with the butter cream and reassemble. Stand the cake on a wire rack with a plate underneath.

Pour the milk into a small saucepan and put over a low heat until it just comes to the boil. Remove from the heat and add the rum and chocolate, broken into small pieces. Stir until the chocolate has melted, returning the pan to a gentle heat, if necessary. Cool the icing, stirring, until it is glossy and coats the back of the wooden spoon thickly. Pour over the cake, place pieces of crystallised ginger in position and leave to set.

Note: If preferred, halve the quantity of icing and ice the top only.

Chocolate and rum dessert cake; Pineapple meringue shortcake; Austrian orange cake

Pineapple meringue shortcake

Metric

250 g plain flour
¼ teaspoon salt
125 g butter
175 g caster sugar
2 standard eggs, separated
1 × 15 ml spoon flaked almonds

For the filling:
396 g can pineapple pieces, drained
125 ml double cream, lightly whipped
Few glacé cherries

Imperial

10 oz plain flour
¼ teaspoon salt
5 oz butter
7 oz caster sugar
2 large eggs, separated
1 tablespoon flaked almonds

For the filling:
14 oz can pineapple pieces, drained
¼ pint double cream, lightly whipped
Few glacé cherries

Cooking Time: 50 minutes
Oven: 190°C, 375°F, Gas Mark 5;
140°C, 275°F, Gas Mark 1

Sieve together the flour and salt. Rub in the butter until the mixture resembles fine breadcrumbs, then add 75 g (3 oz) of the sugar. Blend the egg yolks together. Add to the flour and mix to a stiff dough. Knead lightly on a floured working surface until smooth. Roll out on a greased baking tray to a 23 cm (9 in) circle. Prick with a fork and bake in a moderately hot oven for 20 minutes. Reduce the oven temperature.

Whisk the egg whites until they form stiff peaks. Whisk in the remaining sugar a teaspoon at a time. Spoon tablespoons of the meringue round the edge of the shortcake, or pipe using a large rose nozzle. Sprinkle with the almonds. Return to a cool oven and bake for 30 minutes or until the meringue is crisp. Leave for 10 minutes on the baking tray, then remove and cool on a wire rack.

Fold most of the pineapple into the cream and spread over the centre of the cake. Decorate with the remaining pineapple pieces and cherries.

Hazelnut torte

Metric	Imperial
100 g hazelnuts	*4 oz hazelnuts*
4 standard eggs, separated	*4 large eggs, separated*
125 g caster sugar	*5 oz caster sugar*

For the filling:
50 g unsalted butter
50 g icing sugar, sieved
25 g plain chocolate

For the filling:
2 oz unsalted butter
2 oz icing sugar, sieved
1 oz plain chocolate

For the topping:
75 g granulated sugar
3 × 15 ml spoons water
8 hazelnuts

For the topping:
3 oz granulated sugar
3 tablespoons water
8 hazelnuts

Cooking Time: 30 minutes
Oven: 180°C, 350°F, Gas Mark 4

Grease 2 × 18 cm (7 in) sandwich tins and line the bases and sides with greased greaseproof paper or non-stick silicone paper. Grind the hazelnuts in a blender or coffee grinder. Whisk the egg yolks and sugar until they are thick and creamy. Whisk the egg whites until they form stiff peaks. Fold the ground nuts and egg whites alternately into the egg yolks. Divide the mixture between the two tins and bake in a moderate oven for 30 minutes or until set. Remove the cakes from the oven, leave in the tins for 10 minutes, then turn out on to a wire rack to cool.

Cream the butter and beat in the icing sugar. Melt the chocolate in a basin over a pan of hot water, or in a polythene bag in a bowl of hot water. Beat into the butter and icing sugar. Spread this filling over one of the cakes and sandwich the other one on top.

Put the sugar and water into a small pan and heat gently until the sugar has melted, then boil rapidly until a golden caramel is reached. Using an oiled knife, spread the caramel evenly over the top of the cake. While it is still soft mark into portions with the point of a knife and place the hazelnuts in position.

Coffee gâteau with pears

Metric	Imperial
150 g butter or margarine	*6 oz butter or margarine*
150 g soft brown sugar	*6 oz soft brown sugar*
3 standard eggs, lightly beaten	*3 large eggs, lightly beaten*
175 g self-raising flour	*7 oz self-raising flour*
2 × 15 ml spoons strong black coffee	*2 tablespoons strong black coffee*

For the filling and topping:
1 × 15 ml spoon strong black coffee
2 × 15 ml spoons Tia Maria (optional)
250 ml double cream, lightly whipped
3 ripe dessert pears
1 × 15 ml spoon lemon juice

For the filling and topping:
1 tablespoon strong black coffee
2 tablespoons Tia Maria (optional)
½ pint double cream, lightly whipped
3 ripe dessert pears
1 tablespoon lemon juice

Cooking Time: 20–25 minutes
Oven: 180°C, 350°F, Gas Mark 4

Grease 2 × 18 cm (7 in) sandwich tins and line the bases with greased greaseproof paper. Cream the butter or margarine and sugar until light and fluffy. Gradually beat in the eggs, adding a tablespoon of the flour with the last amount. Sieve in the flour and fold into the creamed mixture. Fold in the coffee. Divide the mixture between the two tins. Level off and bake in a moderate oven for 20–25 minutes. Leave in the tins for 2–3 minutes, then turn out and cool on a wire rack. Fold the coffee and Tia Maria, if using, into the cream. Spread half the cream over one of the cakes. Peel and core the pears, cut into slices and sprinkle with a very little lemon juice to preserve the colour. Put half the pear slices on top of the cream and sandwich the second sponge on top. Spread the remaining cream on top of the cake and arrange the pears attractively.

Gâteau pithiviers; Coffee gâteau with pears; Hazelnut torte

Gâteau pithiviers

Metric	Imperial
200 g puff pastry or use	*8 oz puff pastry or use*
a 368 g packet frozen	*a 13 oz packet frozen*
puff pastry, thawed	*puff pastry, thawed*
100 g blanched almonds,	*4 oz blanched almonds,*
finely chopped	*finely chopped*
75 g caster sugar	*3 oz caster sugar*
50 g butter, softened	*2 oz butter, softened*
2 × 5 ml spoons cornflour	*2 teaspoons cornflour*
2 standard egg yolks	*2 large egg yolks*
1 × 15 ml spoon rum	*1 tablespoon rum*
(optional)	*(optional)*
1 standard egg, beaten	*1 large egg, beaten*
1 × 15 ml spoon icing	*1 tablespoon icing*
sugar, sieved	*sugar, sieved*

Cooking Time: 25 minutes
Oven: 220°C, 425°F, Gas Mark 7

Roll out the pastry and cut into two circles, one 20 cm (8 in) in diameter and the other 23 cm (9 in) in diameter. Place the smaller circle on a damp baking sheet. Mix the almonds with the sugar, butter, cornflour, egg yolks and rum, if using. Spread this mixture on the pastry to within 1.5 cm ($\frac{1}{2}$ in) of the edge. Brush the edge with beaten egg and place the larger pastry circle on top. Seal the edges well, trim them and knock up with the back of a knife. Make criss-cross cuts in the top of the pastry with a sharp knife. Brush all over the top of the pastry with beaten egg and bake in a hot oven for 15 minutes.

Remove from the oven and sprinkle over the icing sugar. Return to the oven and cook for a further 10 minutes. Allow to cool on the baking sheet for 10 minutes, then move to a wire rack and leave until cold.

Children's Christmas house

Metric

For the gingerbread:
150 g butter or margarine
150 g soft brown sugar
1 × 5 ml spoon finely grated lemon rind
1½ × 15 ml spoons lemon juice
100 g black treacle
2 standard eggs, lightly beaten
300 g plain flour
2 × 5 ml spoons baking powder
1 × 15 ml spoon ground ginger
2 × 5 ml spoons ground mixed spice

For the royal icing:
6 standard egg whites
1.8 kg icing sugar, sieved

To decorate:
Smarties, liquorice allsorts, boiled sweets, fruit pastilles, silver balls, hundreds and thousands, little biscuits, etc.
Icing sugar, sieved

Imperial

For the gingerbread:
6 oz butter or margarine
6 oz soft brown sugar
1 teaspoon finely grated lemon rind
1½ tablespoons lemon juice
4 oz black treacle
2 large eggs, lightly beaten
12 oz plain flour
2 teaspoons baking powder
1 tablespoon ground ginger
2 teaspoons ground mixed spice

For the royal icing:
6 large egg whites
4 lb icing sugar, sieved

To decorate:
Smarties, liquorice allsorts, boiled sweets, fruit pastilles, silver balls, hundreds and thousands, little biscuits, etc.
Icing sugar, sieved

Cooking Time: 10 minutes
Oven: 190°C, 375°F, Gas Mark 5

First cut out the shapes of the house in thin card or thick paper. Make two side walls 11 × 20 cm (4½ × 8 in); two end walls 11 × 13 cm (4½ × 5 in) plus a triangular gable, 8 cm (3 in) on each side; and two rectangles for the roof 11 × 23 cm (4½ × 9 in).

Cream the butter and sugar until light and fluffy. Stir in the lemon rind and juice and the treacle. Gradually beat in the eggs. Sieve the flour, baking powder, ginger and spice and stir into the creamed mixture. Place the dough on a lightly floured surface and knead lightly. If you find it is too soft to roll out, wrap in greaseproof paper and chill in the refrigerator for an hour. Divide into 6 portions, two slightly larger than the others. Roll out each of the 4 small portions to the approximate sizes of the pieces of card or paper for the walls. Place the card or paper template on top and cut round. Remove the card or paper and lift the gingerbread carefully on to the greased baking trays. Roll out the 2 larger pieces for the roof as above. (Any trimmings left over can be made into ginger biscuits or gingerbread men.) Bake the gingerbread for about 10 minutes in a moderately hot oven or until crisp. Leave on the baking trays for a few minutes, then carefully place on wire racks to cool. Leave overnight to harden.

Lightly whisk 2 egg whites, then add one-third of the sugar a little at a time, beating well between each addition until the icing is smooth and stands in firm peaks. Spread or pipe, using a plain icing pipe, a line of icing on a cake board or tray and press in one of the side walls so that it sticks firmly and stands upright. If necessary, spread or pipe a little extra icing along either side to help support it. Take an end wall and ice both the side edges. Spread or pipe a line of icing on the board at right-angles to the first wall and press into position. Repeat this process with the other 2 walls until they are all in position. Leave the walls to harden together for at least 2 hours before trying to put on the roof. Cover the bowl of icing with a clean, damp cloth to prevent it from drying.

Carefully spread or pipe a thick layer of icing on the top of the walls and fix the roof in position – it should overlap the walls to make the eaves. Pipe or spread a little icing along the crest of the roof to hold the two pieces firmly together. Leave the house overnight to set firmly.

To decorate the cake whisk the remaining egg whites and add the sugar as above to make a thick icing. Use this to stick various sweets and biscuits carefully on to the house to make doors and windows. Using an icing bag with a small shell or rose nozzle, pipe round the windows and on the roof as in the photograph. Dust the house all over with sieved icing sugar before serving.

Sam the engine; Racing track cake

Racing track cake

Metric	Imperial
300 g butter	12 oz butter
300 g caster sugar	12 oz caster sugar
6 standard eggs, beaten	6 large eggs, beaten
300 g self-raising flour	12 oz self-raising flour

For the butter icing:	For the butter icing:
150 g butter	6 oz butter
4 × 5 ml spoons finely grated lemon rind	4 teaspoons finely grated lemon rind
300 g icing sugar, sieved	12 oz icing sugar, sieved
A little milk to mix	A little milk to mix
Apricot jam, sieved	Apricot jam, sieved

For the fondant icing:	For the fondant icing:
50 g butter	2 oz butter
5 × 15 ml spoons lemon juice	6 tablespoons lemon juice
Food colourings	Food colourings
800 g icing sugar, sieved	2 lb icing sugar, sieved

Cooking Time: 45 minutes–1 hour
Oven: 180°C, 350°F, Gas Mark 4

Grease a 15 cm (6 in) round and a 15 cm (6 in) square cake tin. Make up the basic Victoria Sandwich mixture and bake in a moderate oven for 45 minutes–1 hour or until the cakes spring back when lightly pressed. Leave in the tins for 5 minutes then turn out and cool.

Cream the butter for the butter icing and gradually beat in the lemon rind, icing sugar and enough milk to give a soft spreading consistency. Split the cakes in half, divide most of the icing between them and sandwich together again. Divide the round cake in half to make two semi-circles, spread the remaining butter icing on the cut ends and place on opposite ends of the square cake to form an oval. Place on a cake board and brush all over with apricot jam.

Put the butter and lemon juice for the fondant icing into a pan and heat gently until the butter has just melted. Stir in enough green colouring to turn the mixture a strong green. Add 200 g (8 oz) of the icing sugar and stir the mixture over a low heat, without letting it simmer, until all the sugar has dissolved. Bring the mixture up to simmering point and let it simmer gently for 2 minutes. Remove the pan from the heat and stir in another 200 g (8 oz) icing sugar, beating well with a wooden spoon. Pour the mixture into a bowl and add enough of the remaining sugar, a tablespoon at a time, to make it the consistency of a soft, moulding paste. Sprinkle a working surface liberally with the remaining icing sugar and knead the paste until it is smooth. Work in more green colouring at this stage if necessary.

Roll out three-quarters of the icing to an oval large enough to cover the cake completely. Wrap over the rolling pin and place carefully over the cake. Trim the edges and press the icing into the sides of the cake, smoothing creases.

Colour the remainder of the icing brown, using a little red and yellow colouring, and use to make the fence and track as shown in the photograph. Stick on to the cake using apricot jam. Decorate the top of the cake with racing flags, starting gates and toy racing cars.

Sam the engine

Metric	Imperial
4 standard eggs	4 large eggs
100 g caster sugar	4 oz caster sugar
75 g self-raising flour	3 oz self-raising flour
25 g cocoa powder	1 oz cocoa powder
Cornflour for dredging	Cornflour for dredging

For the butter icing:
100 g butter	4 oz butter
150 g icing sugar, sieved	6 oz icing sugar, sieved
A little milk	A little milk

For the chocolate icing:
8 × 15 ml spoons evaporated milk	9 tablespoons evaporated milk
150 g plain chocolate	6 oz plain chocolate
A little cotton wool	A little cotton wool

For the glacé icing:
100 g icing sugar, sieved	4 oz icing sugar, sieved
A little water	A little water

Cooking Time: 12 minutes
Oven: 200°C, 400°F, Gas Mark 6

Grease a 33 × 20 cm (13 × 8 in) swiss roll tin and a 20 cm (8 in) square shallow cake tin and line the bases and sides of both with greased greaseproof paper. Whisk the eggs and sugar until they are light and creamy and the whisk leaves a trail when it is lifted out. Sieve in the flour and cocoa, then fold into the mixture. Put just over a quarter of the mixture in the 20 cm (8 in) cake tin and the remainder into the swiss roll tin. Level off the mixtures. Bake in a moderately hot oven for 8–12 minutes. If you bake the smaller cake above the larger one, it should take only about 8 minutes, while the swiss roll will take about 12 minutes. This will give you time to cut and roll up the miniature swiss rolls from the smaller cake while the larger cake is still cooking.

Turn the 20 cm (8 in) square cake on to a piece of greaseproof paper dredged with a very little cornflour. Trim the edges and cut the cake in half. Cut one of these halves in half and quickly roll up both quarters in pieces of the greaseproof paper, using the paper as the 'filling'. Cut the remaining half into two rectangles with one slightly larger than the other. Roll up the smaller one as above, but leave the larger one flat.

Turn the cake in the swiss roll tin out on to a piece of cornflour-dredged greaseproof paper, trim the edges and roll up, using the greaseproof paper as the 'filling'. Allow the cakes to cool.

Cream the butter and icing sugar together and beat in a few drops of milk to give a soft spreading consistency. Unroll the large swiss roll, spread with just over half the butter icing, then re-roll and place on a tin or board. Unroll and fill the three small swiss rolls. Cut each of the larger rolls into four for the wheels and stick into position on the cake with a little butter icing. Cut a small slice off the remaining small swiss roll and stick this into the centre of the roll for the button; put the larger piece at the front for the funnel. Cut the remaining rectangle into three pieces and sandwich together with butter icing. Spread the base with a little more icing and put into position at the back of the engine for the hopper. Put the cake into the refrigerator for at least an hour for the butter icing to harden. Remove, place on a wire rack and using a fine pastry brush, brush off any crumbs. Place a tray underneath to catch drips of chocolate icing.

Bring the evaporated milk to the boil in a small saucepan. Remove from the heat, add the chocolate, broken into small pieces and stir until it has melted; if necessary return the pan to a very gentle heat. Allow the mixture to cool, stirring frequently until it is thick and glossy. Carefully spoon the icing all over the cake and leave until it has set. Place a little cotton wool on the funnel for the steam.

Blend the icing sugar with a very little cold water to give a fairly stiff piping icing. Put into a piping bag with a medium-sized writing nozzle and pipe lines on to the engine. Leave until set.

Note: Do not put candles on the cake near the front as the cotton wool could catch fire.

Scones are at their best when fresh and eaten on the same day they are made. This is no great problem as they only take a few minutes to make. They also deep-freeze well. Day-old scones can be refreshed by placing them in a moderate oven for 5 minutes to warm through.

Scones can be made with either self-raising or plain flour. With plain flour add either baking powder or cream of tartar and bicarbonate of soda, as directed in the recipe. The dough for scones should be softer than a pastry dough, but not sticky, and it should be lightly kneaded on a floured surface until smooth. Do not over-knead or the dough will become tough.

For drop scones and Welsh cakes it is important that the griddle or frying pan is at the correct temperature. If it is too hot the dough will burn before it is ready to be turned; if it is too cool the mixture will rise incompletely and be heavy. It is therefore important to test the heat of the griddle first with a small piece of dough. Old-fashioned griddles are not easily found nowadays, and the genuine old ones are expensive, but a thick frying pan can be used equally well.

Teabreads, sliced and spread with butter, are delicious and economical for tea-time or to serve with coffee.

Scones

Metric	Imperial
200 g plain flour	8 oz plain flour
½ teaspoon salt	½ teaspoon salt
1 × 5 ml spoon bicarbonate of soda	1 teaspoon bicarbonate of soda
2 × 5 ml spoons cream of tartar	2 teaspoons cream of tartar
45 g margarine	1½ oz margarine
About 125 ml milk	About ¼ pint milk

Cooking Time: 10 minutes
Oven: 220°C, 425°F, Gas Mark 7

Sieve the flour, salt, bicarbonate of soda and cream of tartar into a bowl. Rub in the margarine until the mixture resembles fine breadcrumbs. Add enough milk to form into a soft but not sticky dough, using a round-bladed knife to mix. Turn on to a floured surface and knead very lightly. Roll out the dough 1.5 cm (½ in) thick. Cut into rounds using a 5 cm (2 in) pastry cutter. Place on lightly-floured baking sheets, sprinkle with a little extra flour and bake in a hot oven for 10 minutes or until risen and golden. Serve warm or cold with butter and jam or cream and jam.
Makes about 8
Variations
Fruit scones: Add 50 g (2 oz) sultanas or currants and 25 g (1 oz) sugar after rubbing in the fat.
Cheese scones: Sieve 1 × 5 ml spoon (1 teaspoon) dry mustard with the flour. Add 75 g (3 oz) finely-grated Cheddar cheese after rubbing in the fat.

Wholemeal scone round with yogurt

Metric	Imperial
200 g wholemeal flour	8 oz wholemeal flour
½ teaspoon salt	½ teaspoon salt
1½ × 5 ml spoons baking powder	1½ teaspoons baking powder
25 g margarine	1 oz margarine
125 ml natural yogurt at room temperature	¼ pint natural yogurt at room temperature

Cooking Time: 15–20 minutes
Oven: 200°C, 400°F, Gas Mark 6

Mix the flour, salt and baking powder. Rub in the margarine. Add the yogurt and mix to a soft dough adding a little extra milk if necessary. Knead lightly on a floured surface, then form into a circle about 18 cm (7 in) in diameter. Place on a greased and floured baking sheet and score into 8 sections. Bake in a moderately hot oven for 15–20 minutes or until risen and golden brown. Cool on a wire rack. Serve with butter and jam.

Scones; Wholemeal scone round with yogurt

Welsh cakes

Metric	Imperial
200 g self-raising flour	8 oz self-raising flour
½ teaspoon salt	½ teaspoon salt
½ teaspoon grated nutmeg	½ teaspoon grated nutmeg
100 g lard or margarine	4 oz lard or margarine
100 g caster sugar	4 oz caster sugar
50 g currants or sultanas	2 oz currants or sultanas
1 standard egg, lightly beaten	1 large egg, lightly beaten
A little milk	A little milk

Cooking Time: 10 minutes

Sieve together the flour, salt and nutmeg. Rub in the lard or margarine until the mixture resembles fine breadcrumbs. Add the sugar and currants or sultanas. Stir in the beaten egg and mix to a stiff dough, adding a very little milk if necessary. Place on a floured surface, knead lightly and roll out to 6 mm (¼ in) thick. Cut into rounds with a 6 cm (2½ in) pastry cutter.

Thoroughly grease a griddle or thick frying pan and heat, testing the temperature as described on page 52 so that the dough browns evenly in about 5 minutes. Place as many of the rounds as you can on the griddle or pan, allowing room for them to spread, and cook for 5 minutes or until evenly browned. Turn over with a palette knife or fish slice and cook for 5 minutes on the other side. Serve warm, spread with butter.

Makes about 16

Potato scones

Metric	Imperial
150 g plain flour	6 oz plain flour
2 × 5 ml spoons baking powder	2 teaspoons baking powder
½ teaspoon salt	½ teaspoon salt
50 g margarine	2 oz margarine
100 g mashed potato	4 oz mashed potato
About 1½ × 15 ml spoons milk	About 2 tablespoons milk
Beaten egg for glazing	Beaten egg for glazing

Cooking Time: about 10 minutes
Oven: 220°C, 425°F, Gas Mark 7

Sieve together the flour, baking powder and salt. Rub in the margarine. Add the potato and mix well, then sufficient milk to make a soft dough; the amount required will depend on how soft the potato is.

Turn on to a floured surface and knead lightly. Roll out 1.5 cm (½ in) thick and cut triangles. Place on greased and floured baking sheets and brush the top of each scone with a little beaten egg. Bake in a hot oven for about 10 minutes or until golden brown and well risen.

Makes about 10

Drop scones

Metric	Imperial
200 g plain flour	8 oz plain flour
1½ × 5 ml spoons baking powder	1½ teaspoons baking powder
½ teaspoon salt	½ teaspoon salt
1 × 15 ml spoon caster sugar	1 tablespoon caster sugar
1 standard egg	1 large egg
About 250 ml milk	About ½ pint milk

Cooking Time: about 4 minutes

Sieve the flour, baking powder, salt and sugar. Make a well in the centre, add the egg and just over half the milk and mix to a smooth batter. Gradually beat in the remaining milk to make a thick batter. Well grease a griddle or thick frying pan and heat, testing as described on page 52. Drop tablespoonfuls of the batter on to the griddle. Cook for about 2 minutes or until the top is covered with bubbles, then turn with a palette knife and cook for a further 2 minutes on the other side. Put the scones inside a clean, folded tea towel to keep warm until they are all cooked, then serve warm with butter and jam or honey.
Makes about 20

Norfolk scone

Metric	Imperial
400 g self-raising flour	1 lb self-raising flour
1 × 5 ml spoon salt	1 teaspoon salt
100 g margarine	4 oz margarine
1 standard egg, lightly beaten	1 large egg, lightly beaten
200 ml milk	Scant ½ pint milk

For the filling and topping:	For the filling and topping:
25 g softened butter or margarine	1 oz softened butter or margarine
100 g currants	4 oz currants
½ teaspoon grated nutmeg	½ teaspoon grated nutmeg
100 g demerara sugar	4 oz demerara sugar
A little milk	A little milk

Cooking Time: about 45 minutes
Oven: 200°C, 400°F, Gas Mark 6

Sieve together the flour and salt. Rub in the margarine. Add the egg and enough milk to mix to a soft but not sticky dough. Turn on to a floured surface and knead lightly. Cut the dough in two and roll each piece out to a 20 cm (8 in) circle. Place one circle on a greased and floured baking sheet. Spread with the butter or margarine. Mix together the currants, nutmeg and almost all the sugar. Sprinkle over the butter. Cover with the second scone round. Brush all over the top of the scone with milk and sprinkle with the remaining sugar. Mark the scone into 8–10 wedges. Bake in a moderately hot oven for about 45 minutes or until well risen and golden brown. Remove from the oven, allow to cool for 10 minutes and serve while still warm.

Potato scones; Norfolk scone; Drop scones; Welsh cakes

Apple scone round

Apple scone round

Metric	Imperial
200 g plain flour	8 oz plain flour
½ teaspoon salt	½ teaspoon salt
2 × 5 ml spoons baking powder	2 teaspoons baking powder
50 g margarine	2 oz margarine
50 g caster sugar	2 oz caster sugar
1 medium-sized cooking apple, peeled, cored and coarsely grated	1 medium-sized cooking apple, peeled, cored and coarsely grated
3 × 15 ml spoons milk	4 tablespoons milk

To glaze:
A little milk
1 × 15 ml spoon demerara sugar

To glaze:
A little milk
1 tablespoon demerara sugar

Cooking Time: 20–25 minutes
Oven: 200°C, 400°F, Gas Mark 6

Sieve together the flour, salt and baking powder. Rub in the margarine. Add the sugar, then the grated apple and add enough milk to give a soft but not sticky dough. Turn the mixture on to a floured surface and knead lightly. Roll out to a 20 cm (8 in) circle and place on a greased and floured baking sheet. Score the scone into 8 pieces. Brush all over the top with milk and sprinkle with the sugar. Bake in a moderately hot oven for 20–25 minutes or until well risen and golden brown. Remove from the oven and cool for 10 minutes, then serve warm with butter.

American muffins

American muffins

Metric	Imperial
150 g plain flour	6 oz plain flour
2 × 5 ml spoons baking powder	2 teaspoons baking powder
25 g caster sugar	1 oz caster sugar
½ teaspoon salt	½ teaspoon salt
1 standard egg, beaten	1 large egg, beaten
125 ml milk	¼ pint milk
4 × 15 ml spoons corn oil	4 tablespoons corn oil

Cooking Time: 25 minutes
Oven: 200°C, 400°F, Gas Mark 6

Well grease 14–16 deep patty tins. Sieve together the flour, baking powder, sugar and salt. Add the egg, milk and oil and beat to a smooth batter. Spoon the mixture into the greased patty tins so that they are two-thirds full. Bake in a moderately hot oven for 25 minutes or until golden brown. Allow to cool for about 5 minutes, then split and serve warm with butter and jam.
Makes 14–16

Barm brack

Metric

375 ml strained cold tea,
saved from the teapot
175 g soft brown sugar
250 g sultanas
50 g chopped mixed peel
250 g self-raising flour
1 standard egg, beaten

Imperial

¾ pint strained cold tea,
saved from the teapot
7 oz soft brown sugar
10 oz sultanas
2 oz chopped mixed peel
10 oz self-raising flour
1 large egg, beaten

Cooking Time: 1¾ hours   Oven: 180°C, 350°F, Gas Mark 4

Put the tea, sugar, sultanas and peel into a bowl. Cover and leave to soak overnight.

Well grease and flour a 20 cm (8 in) round cake tin. Sieve the flour into the fruit mixture, add the egg and beat well. Turn into the cake tin and bake in a moderate oven for 1¾ hours. Leave in the tin for 5 minutes, then turn out and cool on a wire rack. Serve thickly sliced and spread with butter.

Date and walnut loaf

Metric

200 g self-raising flour
1 × 5 ml spoon baking
powder
50 g soft margarine
1 × 15 ml spoon golden
syrup
50 g dates, chopped
50 g walnuts, chopped
6 × 15 ml spoons milk

Imperial

8 oz self-raising flour
1 teaspoon baking
powder
2 oz soft margarine
1 tablespoon golden
syrup
2 oz dates, chopped
2 oz walnuts, chopped
7 tablespoons milk

Cooking Time: 1 hour   Oven: 190°C, 375°F, Gas Mark 5

Well grease a 400 g (1 lb) loaf tin. Sieve the flour and baking powder into a bowl. Add all the remaining ingredients and beat well for 1 minute. Turn into the prepared tin and level off. Bake in a moderately hot oven for about 1 hour or until well risen and a skewer inserted into the centre of the loaf comes out clean. Leave in the tin for 2–3 minutes, then turn out and cool on a wire rack. Serve sliced and spread with butter.

Brazil and apricot loaf

Metric

200 g self-raising flour
¼ teaspoon salt
½ teaspoon grated nutmeg
100 g butter or margarine
100 g dried apricots,
roughly chopped
50 g Brazil nuts, roughly
chopped
75 g soft brown sugar
2 standard eggs, lightly
beaten
About 4 × 15 ml spoons
milk

Imperial

8 oz self-raising flour
¼ teaspoon salt
½ teaspoon grated nutmeg
4 oz butter or margarine
4 oz dried apricots,
roughly chopped
2 oz Brazil nuts, roughly
chopped
3 oz soft brown sugar
2 large eggs, lightly
beaten
About 5 tablespoons
milk

Cooking Time: 1 hour   Oven: 180°C, 350°F, Gas Mark 4

Grease a 400 g (1 lb) loaf tin. Sieve together the flour, salt and nutmeg. Rub in the butter or margarine until the mixture resembles fine breadcrumbs. Add the apricots, Brazil nuts and sugar. Make a well in the centre, pour in the eggs and the milk and mix to a soft dropping consistency, adding a little extra milk if necessary. Turn into the prepared tin and level off. Bake in a moderate oven for 1 hour or until a skewer inserted into the centre comes out clean. Leave in the tin for 5 minutes, then turn out and cool on a wire rack. Slice and spread with butter to serve.

Date and walnut loaf; Brazil and apricot loaf; Cottage cheese and walnut tea bread; Barm brack

Cottage cheese and walnut tea bread

Metric

200 g cottage cheese, sieved
125 g soft brown sugar
3 standard eggs, beaten
75 g walnuts, chopped
50 g chopped mixed peel
(optional)
200 g self-raising flour
1 × 5 ml spoon baking
powder
½ teaspoon salt

Imperial

8 oz cottage cheese, sieved
5 oz soft brown sugar
3 large eggs, beaten
3 oz walnuts, chopped
2 oz chopped mixed peel
(optional)
8 oz self-raising flour
1 teaspoon baking
powder
½ teaspoon salt

Cooking Time: 1 hour   Oven: 180°C, 350°F, Gas Mark 4

Well grease and flour a 600 g (1½ lb) loaf tin. Cream together the cottage cheese and sugar and beat in the eggs. Stir in the walnuts and peel if used. Sieve in the flour, baking powder and salt and fold into the mixture. Turn into the prepared tin. Bake in a moderate oven for 1 hour until well risen and golden brown. Leave in the tin for 5 minutes then turn out and cool on a wire rack. Serve sliced and spread with butter.

Cheese and date bread

Metric

200 g plain flour
1 × 5 ml spoon salt
2 × 5 ml spoons dry
mustard
4 × 5 ml spoons baking
powder
200 g wholemeal flour
75 g butter or margarine
200 g Cheddar cheese,
finely grated
150 g dates, stoned and
chopped
2 standard eggs, lightly
beaten
250 ml milk

Imperial

8 oz plain flour
1 teaspoon salt
2 teaspoons dry
mustard
4 teaspoons baking
powder
8 oz wholemeal flour
3 oz butter or margarine
8 oz Cheddar cheese,
finely grated
6 oz dates, stoned and
chopped
2 large eggs, lightly
beaten
½ pint milk

Cooking Time: 1 hour   Oven: 190°C, 375°F, Gas Mark 5

Well grease an 800 g (2 lb) loaf tin. Sieve together the plain flour, salt, mustard and baking powder. Add the wholemeal flour and rub in the butter or margarine. Add the cheese and dates and mix well. Add the eggs and milk and mix to a soft dough. Turn into the prepared tin and level off. Bake in a moderately hot oven for 1 hour or until well risen and golden brown. Leave in the tin for a few minutes, then turn out and cool on a wire rack. Serve sliced and spread with butter.

Cheese and date bread; Cheese and celery loaf

Wiltshire tea bread

Metric	Imperial
150 g unsmoked streaky bacon	6 oz unsmoked streaky bacon
3 sticks celery, finely chopped	3 sticks celery, finely chopped
1 small onion, peeled and very finely chopped	1 small onion, peeled and very finely chopped
400 g self-raising flour	1 lb self-raising flour
Pinch of salt	Pinch of salt
Freshly ground black pepper	Freshly ground black pepper
50 g lard or dripping	2 oz lard or dripping
1 × 15 ml spoon finely chopped parsley	1 tablespoon finely chopped parsley
Generous 125 ml milk	Generous ¼ pint milk
1 standard egg, beaten	1 large egg, beaten

Cooking Time: 1 hour   Oven: 190°C, 375°F, Gas Mark 5

Well grease an 800 g (2 lb) loaf tin. Cut off the rind and chop bacon finely. Put into a pan, heat gently until the fat runs, then cook for 2 minutes. Add the celery and onion and cook gently for a further 5 minutes. Allow to cool. Sieve the flour, salt (unless the bacon is very salty) and a little pepper. Rub in the lard or dripping. Add the bacon mixture and the parsley, then the milk and beaten egg and mix to a soft dough. Knead lightly on a floured surface, shape into a rectangle and place in the prepared tin. Bake in a moderately hot oven for 1 hour. Remove from the tin and allow to cool for at least 15 minutes on a wire rack. Serve warm or cold, spread with butter.

Cheese and celery loaf

Metric	Imperial
250 g self-raising flour	10 oz self-raising flour
1 × 5 ml spoon salt	1 teaspoon salt
50 g butter or margarine	2 oz butter or margarine
2 sticks celery, finely chopped	2 sticks celery, finely chopped
100 g Cheshire cheese, grated	4 oz Cheshire cheese, grated
1 small clove garlic, crushed	1 small clove garlic, crushed
1 standard egg, beaten	1 large egg, beaten
100 ml milk	¼ pint milk

Cooking Time: 1 hour   Oven: 190°C, 375°F, Gas Mark 5

Well grease a 400 g (1 lb) loaf tin. Sieve together the flour and salt. Rub in the butter or margarine. Add the celery, cheese and garlic and mix well. Add the egg and milk and mix to a soft dough. Knead lightly with your hands in the bowl, form into an oblong and place in the prepared tin. Bake in a moderately hot oven for 1 hour or until golden brown and well risen. Leave in the tin for a few minutes, then turn out on to a wire rack. Serve warm or cold, sliced with butter. This bread is particularly good served with a vegetable soup.

Yeast cookery is often thought of as being very complicated and difficult. In reality it is no harder than any other form of baking, and much easier than most people imagine. The old idea that bread had to be proved (left to rise) in a warm place has now been discredited, as it has been found that it will rise equally well at low temperatures, although more slowly.

For most yeasted breads the method consists of just a few basic steps. First the yeast is dissolved in hand-hot water or milk – about 43°C (110°F) – and left in a warm place for about 10 minutes or until it has become frothy. Fresh yeast is becoming increasingly difficult to buy, so in all these recipes dried yeast has been used. This works just as well and can easily be bought in supermarkets, grocers, chemists and health food shops. It has the added advantage that it can be kept in a storecupboard for several months. When the yeast liquid is frothy it is added to the flour and mixed to a dough. Although you can use ordinary plain flour for bread-making, it is better to use a strong plain flour, which is made with harder wheat and has greater elasticity.

The dough then has to be kneaded for about 10 minutes, until it becomes smooth and elastic. If you have an electric mixer with a dough hook, use this; if not knead it by hand. Place the dough on a lightly-floured surface and knead by folding the dough towards you with your fingers, then push down and away with the palm of the hand. Give the dough a quarter turn and repeat this motion, developing a rocking movement.

After kneading the dough is put into a large lightly-oiled polythene bag, or into a clean mixing bowl covered with a clean damp cloth and left to prove until it has doubled in size. For a dough made with 600 g (1½ lb) flour this will take about 45–60 minutes in a warm place such as on top of the cooker when the oven is in use, or in an airing cupboard. If you want a quick rise be careful not to put the dough in *too* hot a place, such as an oven warming drawer which has elements in the bottom, as this will kill the yeast and prevent it from rising. For a slower rise, leave the dough at room temperature, in which case it will take about 2 hours, or alternatively it can be left for about 12 hours in a cold larder or refrigerator. If proved in this way it must be allowed to return to room temperature before it is shaped.

It is also possible to leave the dough in the refrigerator for 6 hours, then take it out and leave it at room temperature or in a warm place to finish.

After the first proving the dough is kneaded again for a minute, to knock out all the air bubbles, and then shaped. After shaping the dough is left to rise again, either in a warm place or at room temperature, until it has doubled in size, and is then baked. To test if a loaf is cooked, carefully remove from the tin, turn upside down and tap with your knuckles – if it is cooked it will sound hollow.

Cool the bread on a wire rack and when it is cold put into a breadbin, wrap in foil or put in a polythene bag.

White bread

White bread

Metric

For the yeast liquid:
1 × 5 ml spoon sugar
375 ml warm water
2 × 5 ml spoons dried yeast

For the dough:
600 g strong plain flour
2 × 5 ml spoons salt
15 g lard or margarine

Imperial

For the yeast liquid:
1 teaspoon sugar
¾ pint warm water
2 teaspoons dried yeast

For the dough:
1½ lb strong plain flour
2 teaspoons salt
½ oz lard or margarine

Cooking Time: 40 minutes
Oven: 220°C, 425°F, Gas Mark 7

Dissolve the sugar in the warm water. Sprinkle over the dried yeast and leave for about 10 minutes or until the mixture is frothy. Sieve the flour and salt and rub in the lard or margarine. Add the yeast liquid to the flour and work to a firm dough which leaves the sides of the bowl clean. Place on a lightly-floured surface and knead the dough thoroughly for about 10 minutes until it feels smooth and elastic. Either replace the dough in the cleaned bowl and cover with a damp cloth, or put into an oiled polythene bag. Leave to prove until the dough has about doubled in size. Replace on the floured surface and knead for about a minute to knock out all the air bubbles. Shape into an oblong and put into a greased 800 g (2 lb) loaf tin, then either re-cover with the damp cloth or replace in the polythene bag. Leave until the dough has risen to just above the top of the tin. Remove the cloth or bag and bake the loaf in a hot oven for about 40 minutes. Cool on a wire rack.
Note: If preferred the dough can be cooked in 2 × 400 g (1 lb) loaf tins for about 30 minutes.

Quick wholemeal bread

Metric	Imperial
For the yeast liquid:	For the yeast liquid:
1 × 5 ml spoon sugar	1 teaspoon sugar
400 ml warm water	Generous ¾ pint warm water
2 × 5 ml spoons dried yeast	2 teaspoons dried yeast
For the dough:	For the dough:
200 g strong plain flour	8 oz strong plain flour
2 × 5 ml spoons salt	2 teaspoons salt
400 g wholemeal flour	1 lb wholemeal flour
2 × 15 ml spoons oil	2 tablespoons oil
To glaze:	To glaze:
Salt water	Salt water
Cracked wheat or coarse oatmeal	Cracked wheat or coarse oatmeal

Cooking Time: 30–40 minutes
Oven: 220°C, 425°F, Gas Mark 7

Dissolve the sugar in the water in a bowl. Sprinkle over the dried yeast and leave in a warm place for 10 minutes until frothy. Sieve the plain flour and salt together and add the wholemeal flour. Add the oil to the yeast liquid, pour into the flour and mix to a soft dough. Place on a lightly-floured surface and knead the dough for 10 minutes or until it feels smooth and elastic. Divide the dough in half and form into two balls. Place on greased and floured baking sheets. Brush all over the loaves with a little salt water and sprinkle with cracked wheat or oatmeal.
Either put the baking sheets into large polythene bags or cover the loaves with a damp cloth. Leave to rise until double their original size. Bake in a hot oven for 30–40 minutes. Remove from the sheets and cool on a wire rack.
Makes 2 loaves

Onion bread

Metric	Imperial
For the yeast liquid:	For the yeast liquid:
½ teaspoon sugar	½ teaspoon sugar
125 ml warm water	¼ pint warm water
1 × 5 ml spoon dried yeast	1 teaspoon dried yeast
For the dough:	For the dough:
200 g strong plain flour	8 oz strong plain flour
½ teaspoon salt	½ teaspoon salt
1 × 15 ml spoon corn oil	1 tablespoon corn oil
For the onion topping:	For the onion topping:
40 g butter	1½ oz butter
300 g Spanish onions, peeled and cut into rings	12 oz Spanish onions, peeled and cut into rings
Salt and freshly ground black pepper	Salt and freshly ground black pepper
½ teaspoon poppy seeds	½ teaspoon poppy seeds

Cooking Time: 40–45 minutes
Oven: 190°C, 375°F, Gas Mark 5

Dissolve the sugar in the warm water, sprinkle over the dried yeast and leave in a warm place for about 10 minutes or until frothy. Sieve together the flour and salt. Add the yeast liquid and oil and mix to a soft dough. Turn on to a lightly-floured surface and knead for 10 minutes or until the dough feels smooth and elastic. Put into an oiled polythene bag or a clean bowl and cover with a damp cloth. Leave to rise until the dough has doubled in size.
While the dough is rising melt the butter in a pan and fry the onions very gently for 15 minutes or until golden. Season to taste with salt and pepper.
Grease a 20 cm (8 in) sandwich tin. Turn the risen dough on to a floured surface and knead for a minute. Roll out to a 20 cm (8 in) circle and place in the tin. Spoon over the onions and sprinkle with the poppy seeds. Leave in a warm place until the dough has doubled in size. Bake in a moderately hot oven for 40–45 minutes or until the top is golden brown. Serve warm or cold.

Oatmeal bread

Metric	Imperial
For the dough:	**For the dough:**
200 g medium oatmeal	*8 oz medium oatmeal*
250 ml milk	*½ pint milk*
300 g strong plain flour	*12 oz strong plain flour*
1½ × 5 ml spoons salt	*1½ teaspoons salt*
2 × 15 ml spoons corn oil	*2 tablespoons corn oil*
For the yeast liquid:	**For the yeast liquid:**
1 × 5 ml spoon sugar	*1 teaspoon sugar*
4 × 15 ml spoons warm water	*4 tablespoons warm water*
2 × 5 ml spoons dried yeast	*2 teaspoons dried yeast*
To glaze:	**To glaze:**
A little milk	*A little milk*
1 × 15 ml spoon medium or coarse oatmeal	*1 tablespoon medium or coarse oatmeal*

Cooking Time: 1 hour
Oven: 220°C, 425°F, Gas Mark 7;
150°C, 300°F, Gas Mark 2

Put the oatmeal into a basin, pour over the milk and leave to soak for 30 minutes. Dissolve the sugar in the warm water, sprinkle over the yeast and leave in a warm place for about 10 minutes or until frothy. Sieve the flour and salt into a bowl. Make a well in the centre, add the oatmeal, yeast liquid and oil and mix to a soft dough. Turn on to a floured surface and knead for about 10 minutes until the dough feels smooth and elastic. Place the dough in an oiled polythene bag or a bowl and cover with a damp cloth. Leave to rise until the dough has doubled in size.

Grease 2 × 400 g (1 lb) loaf tins. Turn the dough on to a floured working surface and knead for 1–2 minutes. Divide the dough in half and shape into two rectangles. Place in the prepared loaf tins, brush the tops of the loaves with milk and sprinkle with oatmeal. Cover with a damp cloth or replace inside the bag and leave to rise until the dough has doubled in size. Bake in a hot oven for 30 minutes, then lower the temperature and bake for a further 30 minutes. Turn out of the tins and cool on a wire rack. This bread will keep moist and fresh for several days and is also good toasted.

Oatmeal bread; Onion bread; Quick wholemeal bread

Crumpets

Metric	Imperial
1 × 5 ml spoon sugar	*1 teaspoon sugar*
625 ml warm milk	*1¼ pints warm milk*
2 × 5 ml spoons dried yeast	*2 teaspoons dried yeast*
400 g plain flour	*1 lb plain flour*
1 × 5 ml spoon salt	*1 teaspoon salt*
½ teaspoon bicarbonate of soda	*½ teaspoon bicarbonate of soda*

Cooking Time: 12 minutes

Dissolve the sugar in the milk, sprinkle over the dried yeast and leave for about 10 minutes in a warm place until frothy. Sieve the flour, salt and bicarbonate of soda into a bowl. Add half the yeast liquid and beat well, then gradually beat in the remaining liquid to give a thin batter. Beat well, cover the bowl with a cloth and leave in a warm place until the batter has doubled in size.

Well grease a griddle or thick frying pan and several 8 cm (3 in) crumpet rings (or use pastry cutters or poaching rings). Heat the griddle or pan and test as described on page 52. Pour 2 tablespoons of the batter into each ring in the pan. Reduce the heat after about 4 minutes and cook the crumpets for a further 6 minutes. Remove the rings and turn the crumpets over to cook on the other side for 2–3 minutes. Serve the crumpets hot, toasted on both sides and thickly spread with butter.

Makes about 15

Crumpets

Devonshire splits

Metric

For the yeast liquid:
1 × 5 ml spoon sugar
125 ml mixed warm milk and water
2 × 5 ml spoons dried yeast

For the dough:
200 g strong plain flour
½ teaspoon salt
25 g butter or margarine

For the filling:
Strawberry jam
125 ml clotted cream or whipped double cream

Imperial

For the yeast liquid:
1 teaspoon sugar
¼ pint mixed warm milk and water
2 teaspoons dried yeast

For the dough:
8 oz strong plain flour
½ teaspoon salt
1 oz butter or margarine

For the filling:
Strawberry jam
¼ pint clotted cream or whipped double cream

Cooking Time: 15 minutes
Oven: 220°C, 425°F, Gas Mark 7

Dissolve the sugar in the milk, sprinkle over the dried yeast and leave in a warm place for about 10 minutes or until frothy. Sieve together the flour and salt. Rub in the butter or margarine. Pour in the yeast liquid and mix to a soft dough. Turn the dough on to a lightly-floured surface and knead for 10 minutes or until it feels smooth and elastic. Put into an oiled polythene bag or a basin covered with a damp cloth and leave to rise until the dough has doubled in size. Replace the dough on the floured surface and knead for a minute. Divide into 8. Form each piece of dough into a ball and place on a greased and floured baking tray. Replace inside the bag or cover with a damp cloth and leave to rise until the balls have doubled in size. Bake in a hot oven for 15 minutes and cool on a wire rack. Before serving split the buns and fill with jam and cream.
Makes 8

Devonshire splits

Croissants

Croissants

Metric	Imperial
For the yeast liquid:	For the yeast liquid:
1 × 5 ml spoon sugar	1 teaspoon sugar
200 ml warm water	7½ fl oz warm water
1 × 15 ml spoon dried yeast	1 tablespoon dried yeast
For the dough:	For the dough:
400 g strong plain flour	1 lb strong plain flour
2 × 5 ml spoons salt	2 teaspoons salt
25 g lard	1 oz lard
1 standard egg, lightly beaten	1 large egg, lightly beaten
150 g butter	6 oz butter
For the egg wash:	For the egg wash:
1 egg	1 egg
2 × 15 ml spoons water	2 tablespoons water
½ teaspoon sugar	½ teaspoon sugar

Cooking Time: about 20 minutes
Oven: 220°C, 425°F, Gas Mark 7

Dissolve the sugar in the water in a basin and sprinkle over the yeast. Leave for 10 minutes or until frothy. Sieve together the flour and salt and rub in the lard. Add the egg and yeast liquid and mix to a dough. Knead well.
Roll the dough out to a rectangle 50 × 15 cm (20 × 6 in) Divide the butter into three. Dot the top two thirds of the dough with one part of the butter as if making flaky pastry, fold the dough in three as in puff pastry and roll (page 80). Repeat using other two parts butter. Rest between rollings.
Repeat the folding and rolling three more times. Put in a polythene bag and leave in a cold place or refrigerator for at least 1 hour. To shape the croissants, roll out the dough to a rectangle slightly larger than 45 × 30 cm (18 × 12 in), cover with oiled polythene or a damp cloth and leave for 10 minutes. Trim the edges and divide in half lengthways. Cut each strip into 3 squares, then each square into 2 triangles.
Beat the egg with the water and sugar. Brush over the triangles. Roll up each triangle loosely towards the point, finishing with the tip underneath. Curve into a crescent. Brush with egg wash and place on ungreased baking sheets. Put inside oiled polythene bags or cover with a damp cloth and leave to rise in a warm place for about 30 minutes until light. Brush again with egg wash. Bake in a hot oven for about 20 minutes or until golden brown.
Makes 12

Muffins

Muffins

Metric	Imperial
1 × 5 ml spoon sugar	1 teaspoon sugar
250 ml warm water	½ pint warm water
2 × 5 ml spoons dried yeast	2 teaspoons dried yeast
400 g strong plain flour	1 lb strong plain flour
1 × 5 ml spoon salt	1 teaspoon salt
25 g butter, melted	1 oz butter, melted

Cooking Time: 10 minutes
Oven: 230°C, 450°F, Gas Mark 8

Dissolve the sugar in the warm water. Sprinkle over the yeast and leave in a warm place for 10 minutes or until frothy. Sieve together the flour and salt. Add the yeast liquid and butter and mix to a soft dough, adding a little extra warm water if necessary. Place on a floured surface and knead for about 10 minutes or until the dough feels smooth and elastic. Put into an oiled polythene bag or a bowl covered with a damp cloth, and leave until the dough has doubled in size.

Knead the dough lightly and roll out until it is just over 6 mm (¼ in) thick. Leave to rest for 5 minutes, covered with a damp cloth, then cut into 8 cm (3 in) rounds. Re-roll the dough and cut out more muffins until it has all been used. Place the muffins on well-floured baking sheets and dust the tops with flour. Replace in the polythene bag or re-cover with a damp cloth and leave to rise until doubled in size. Bake the muffins in a very hot oven for 5 minutes. Remove from the oven, turn all the muffins over with a palette knife, replace in the oven and cook for a further 5 minutes.

To serve, pull the muffins apart all the way round the edge, almost to the centre, with your fingers or with a knife. Toast slowly on both sides. Pull apart, butter each piece well, then put together again and serve hot.
Makes about 14.

Butterscotch ginger buns

Metric

For the yeast liquid:
1 × 5 ml spoon sugar
125 ml warm milk
2 × 5 ml spoons dried yeast

For the dough:
200 g strong plain flour
½ teaspoon salt
25 g butter
1 standard egg, lightly beaten

For the topping:
50 g butter
100 g dark brown sugar
1 × 15 ml spoon golden syrup
50 g crystallised ginger, finely chopped

Imperial

For the yeast liquid:
1 teaspoon sugar
¼ pint warm milk
2 teaspoons dried yeast

For the dough:
8 oz strong plain flour
½ teaspoon salt
1 oz butter
1 large egg, lightly beaten

For the topping:
2 oz butter
4 oz dark brown sugar
1 tablespoon golden syrup
2 oz crystallised ginger, finely chopped

Cooking Time: 30 minutes
Oven: 200°C, 400°F, Gas Mark 6

Dissolve the sugar in the milk, sprinkle over the dried yeast and leave in a warm place for about 10 minutes or until frothy. Sieve together the flour and salt. Rub in the butter. Pour in the yeast liquid and egg and mix to a soft dough. Turn on to a lightly floured surface and knead for 10 minutes or until the dough feels smooth and elastic. Put into an oiled polythene bag or into a bowl and cover with a damp cloth. Leave to rise until the dough has doubled in size.

Put the butter, sugar and syrup into a pan and heat until the butter has melted and the sugar dissolved. Remove from the heat and stir in the ginger. Well grease an 18 cm (7 in) square cake tin and pour in half the ginger mixture, spreading it evenly.

Turn the dough on to a floured surface, knead for a minute then roll out to a rectangle about 35 × 23 cm (14 × 9 in) and spread with the remaining ginger mixture. Roll up from one of the long sides, like a swiss roll, and cut into 9 rolls. Place the rolls in the tin on top of the ginger mixture. Cover with a damp cloth and leave to rise in a warm place until the mixture has doubled in size. Bake in a moderately hot oven for 30 minutes or until the buns are golden. Remove from the oven, allow to cool in the tin for 10 minutes, then turn upside down on to a wire rack. Allow to cool.

Makes 9 buns

Lardy bread

Metric

For the yeast liquid:
1 × 5 ml spoon sugar
250 ml warm water
2 × 5 ml spoons dried yeast

For the dough:
400 g strong plain flour
2 × 5 ml spoons salt
115 g lard
100 g caster sugar
A little milk to glaze

Imperial

For the yeast liquid:
1 teaspoon sugar
½ pint warm water
2 teaspoons dried yeast

For the dough:
1 lb strong plain flour
2 teaspoons salt
4½ oz lard
4 oz caster sugar
A little milk to glaze

Cooking Time: 30 minutes
Oven: 220°C, 425°F, Gas Mark 7

Dissolve the sugar in the water, sprinkle over the yeast and leave for about 10 minutes in a warm place until frothy. Sieve the flour and salt into a bowl. Rub in 15 g (½ oz) of the lard. Add the yeast liquid and mix to a dough that leaves the sides of the bowl clean. Turn on to a lightly-floured surface and knead for 10 minutes or until the dough feels smooth and elastic. Put into an oiled polythene bag or a bowl covered with a damp cloth and leave to rise until the dough has doubled in size.

Turn the dough on to the floured surface and roll out until it is 6 mm (¼ in) thick. Dot one third of the lard in small flakes all over the dough and sprinkle with one third of the sugar. Roll up loosely like a swiss roll. Give the dough a half turn and repeat this process twice more until all the lard and sugar has been used. Roll the dough out to fit a 20 × 25 cm (8 × 10 in) greased shallow baking tin. Press down firmly to fill up the corners. Make a criss-cross pattern on top of the dough using a sharp knife. Replace in the polythene bag or re-cover with a damp cloth and leave to rise again until double in size. Remove bag or cloth.

Brush the dough with the milk and bake in a hot oven for 30 minutes. Leave in the tin for about 5 minutes, then turn out to cool on a wire rack. Serve hot or cold, spread with butter and jam.

Apricot plait; Butterscotch ginger buns; Lardy bread

Apricot plait

Metric

For the yeast liquid:
1 × 5 ml spoon sugar
*200 ml mixed warm milk
and water*
2 × 5 ml spoons dried yeast

For the dough:
300 g strong plain flour
½ teaspoon salt
50 g butter or margarine
*50 g dried apricots,
chopped*
*50 g stoned or seedless
raisins*
*1 × 5 ml spoon finely
grated lemon rind*
*1 standard egg, lightly
beaten*

For the topping:
100 g icing sugar, sieved
*About 1 × 15 ml spoon
water*
*25 g browned flaked
almonds*

Imperial

For the yeast liquid:
1 teaspoon sugar
*7½ fl oz mixed warm milk
and water*
2 teaspoons dried yeast

For the dough:
12 oz strong plain flour
½ teaspoon salt
2 oz butter or margarine
*2 oz dried apricots,
chopped*
*2 oz stoned or seedless
raisins*
*1 teaspoon finely
grated lemon rind*
*1 large egg, lightly
beaten*

For the topping:
4 oz icing sugar, sieved
*About 1 tablespoon
water*
*1 oz browned flaked
almonds*

Cooking Time: 30 minutes
Oven: 220°C, 425°F, Gas Mark 7;
         190°C, 375°F, Gas Mark 5

Dissolve the sugar in the milk and water. Sprinkle over the dried yeast and leave in a warm place for about 10 minutes or until frothy. Sieve the flour and salt into a bowl. Rub in the butter or margarine. Add the apricots, raisins and lemon rind. Mix well. Make a well in the centre, pour in the egg and yeast liquid and mix to a soft dough. Turn on to a lightly floured surface and knead for about 10 minutes or until the dough feels smooth and elastic. Cover with a damp cloth and leave to rest for 5 minutes. Divide the dough into 5 and roll each piece out to a rope about 30 cm (12 in) long. Plait three of these ropes together and place on a greased and floured baking tray. Twist the other two ropes together and place carefully on top.
Cover the loaf with a damp cloth and leave to rise in a warm place until double its original size. Bake in a hot oven for 10 minutes, then reduce the heat and bake for a further 20 minutes, or until the loaf is golden brown and sounds hollow when tapped. Remove from the oven, place on a wire rack and leave to cool.
Blend the icing sugar with enough water to give a thick flowing consistency and spoon over the top of the loaf. Sprinkle with the almonds.

Bara brith

Metric	Imperial
For the yeast liquid:	For the yeast liquid:
1 × 5 ml spoon sugar	1 teaspoon sugar
150 ml warm water	¼ pint plus 2 tablespoons
1 × 15 ml spoon dried	warm water
yeast	1 tablespoon dried yeast
For the dough:	For the dough:
400 g plain flour	1 lb plain flour
1 × 5 ml spoon salt	1 teaspoon salt
1 × 5 ml spoon mixed spice	1 teaspoon mixed spice
75 g margarine	3 oz margarine
75 g demerara sugar	3 oz demerara sugar
500 g mixed dried fruit	1¼ lb mixed dried fruit
1 standard egg beaten	1 large egg, beaten
To glaze:	To glaze:
Honey or syrup	Honey or syrup

Cooking Time: 50–60 minutes
Oven: 180°C, 350°F, Gas Mark 4

Dissolve the sugar in the warm water, sprinkle over the yeast and put on one side for 10 minutes or until frothy. Sieve together the flour, salt and mixed spice. Rub in the margarine and add the sugar and dried fruit. Pour in the yeast liquid together with the beaten egg and mix well until the dough leaves the sides of the bowl clean. Turn out on to a lightly-floured surface and knead for about 10 minutes or until the dough feels smooth and elastic. Place the dough in an oiled polythene bag or a bowl covered with a damp cloth and leave to rise until the dough has doubled in size.

Turn on to a floured surface and knead for 1–2 minutes. Divide the dough in half and shape to fit two greased 400 g (1 lb) loaf tins. Place each tin in an oiled polythene bag or cover with a damp cloth and leave to rise until the dough is above the top of the tins. Bake in a moderate oven for 50–60 minutes. Remove from the oven, turn out on to a wire rack and brush the loaves with honey or syrup while still warm. Serve the loaves thinly sliced and spread with butter.

Almond Christmas wreath

Metric	Imperial
For the yeast batter:	For the yeast batter:
50 g plain flour	2 oz plain flour
1 × 5 ml spoon sugar	1 teaspoon sugar
1 × 5 ml spoon dried yeast	1 teaspoon dried yeast
125 ml warm milk, less	¼ pint warm milk, less
3 × 15 ml spoons	3 tablespoons
For the dough:	For the dough:
150 g plain flour	6 oz plain flour
½ teaspoon salt	½ teaspoon salt
25 g margarine	1 oz margarine
2 × 5 ml spoons finely	2 teaspoons finely grated
grated orange rind	orange rind
1 standard egg, beaten	1 large egg, beaten
For the filling:	For the filling:
50 g ground almonds	2 oz ground almonds
50 g caster sugar	2 oz caster sugar
1 standard egg yolk	1 large egg yolk
For the icing:	For the icing:
100 g icing sugar, sieved	4 oz icing sugar, sieved
About 1 × 15 ml spoon	About 1 tablespoon
orange juice	orange juice
50 g red and green glacé	2 oz red and green glacé
cherries, chopped	cherries, chopped

Cooking Time: 45–50 minutes
Oven: 190°C, 375°F, Gas Mark 5

Blend the flour, sugar, dried yeast and milk together in a bowl and put on one side in a warm place until frothy – about 15 minutes. Sieve the flour and salt into a separate bowl and rub in the margarine. Add the orange rind. Add the yeast mixture and beaten egg and mix to a dough that leaves the sides of the bowl clean.

Turn on to a lightly-floured surface and knead for about 10 minutes until the dough feels smooth and elastic. Place in an oiled polythene bag or a bowl covered with a damp cloth and leave to rise until the dough has doubled in size. Remove and knead lightly on a floured surface for 1 minute. Divide the dough in half. Roll each piece out to a rectangle 30 × 13 cm (12 × 5 in).

Blend the almonds and caster sugar together and bind with the egg yolk to make marzipan. Divide in half. Dust the working surface with a little sieved icing sugar and roll out the marzipan to two rectangles a little smaller than the dough. Place on top of the dough. Roll up lengthways and seal the edge of the dough. Place the two rolls on a greased and floured baking tray, form into a circle and twist the ends together. Replace inside the polythene bag or cover with a damp cloth. Leave to rise in a warm place until doubled in size. Bake in a moderately hot oven for 45–50 minutes or until golden. Remove from the oven and cool on a wire rack.

Stir enough orange juice into the icing sugar to give a thick flowing consistency. Spoon over the wreath and decorate with the glacé cherries.

Bara brith; Gugelhopf; Almond Christmas wreath

Gugelhopf

Metric

2 × 5 ml spoons dried yeast
1 × 15 ml spoon warm water
1 × 5 ml spoon sugar
25 g flaked almonds
150 g plain flour
½ teaspoon salt
50 g margarine
25 g caster sugar
1 egg, beaten
125 ml warm milk
50 g currants

To finish:
Icing sugar

Imperial

2 teaspoons dried yeast
1 tablespoon warm water
1 teaspoon sugar
1 oz flaked almonds
6 oz plain flour
½ teaspoon salt
2 oz margarine
1 oz caster sugar
1 egg, beaten
¼ pint warm milk
2 oz currants

To finish:
Icing sugar

Cooking Time: 45 minutes
Oven: 180°C, 350°F, Gas Mark 4

Blend the yeast with the warm water and teaspoon of sugar and put into a warm place for 5–10 minutes or until frothy. Well grease a 20 cm (8 in) gugelhopf tin with butter and sprinkle over the flaked almonds (if a gugelhopf mould is difficult to obtain, a savarin tin can be used instead). Sieve the flour and salt. Rub in the margarine. Add the sugar. Make a well in the centre, add the egg, yeast mixture and milk. Beat well for 5 minutes to form a smooth batter. Beat in the currants. Pour the mixture into the prepared tin. Cover with a damp cloth and leave to rise in a warm place until the dough reaches the top of the tin, or doubles in size. Bake in a moderate oven for 45 minutes or until golden brown. Remove from the oven, cool for 2–3 minutes in the tin, then turn out and cool on a wire rack. Sprinkle with sieved icing sugar before serving on the day it is made.

Freshly-baked shortcrust tarts, cream buns and layers of light puff pastry with fresh cream make superb tea-time treats without too much effort in the kitchen. If you find puff pastry too time-consuming or difficult to make, the frozen packets are excellent, or you can use some of the very good packet mixes now readily available.

Choux pastry is nothing like as difficult to make as most people imagine. In addition to the recipes given here it can also be used for éclairs, small profiteroles served with chocolate sauce, or small savoury buns filled with prawns, mushrooms in white sauce, chicken etc, and served either hot or cold for an hors d'oeuvre.

Shortcrust pastry forms the basis of so many different recipes, both savoury and sweet, that it is well worth mastering the art of making it. Whether the fat you use is butter, margarine, lard, cooking fat or a mixture is entirely a matter of personal choice and which you find most successful. But there's nothing to beat butter for flavour. Try to have the fat and most of your utensils as cold as possible before you start. Rub the fat into the flour with your fingertips until it really does resemble fine breadcrumbs, as lumps of fat in the finished pastry will tend to stretch it. Do not add too much water as this will make the pastry hard and brittle. Turn the dough on to a lightly-floured surface and knead it very gently – again if you over-handle it will become hard and brittle. Roll out the dough on a floured surface, but do not stretch it, as this will cause it to shrink when baked.

Unbaked shortcrust pastry dough freezes well, so it is practical to make up a large batch at any one time and freeze it. Alternatively the rubbed-in fat and flour can be kept in a covered container in the refrigerator for 2–3 weeks and you can just add water to use it.

Cooked puff pastry can also be frozen, but tends to lose some of its texture. Choux pastry freezes very well – cream buns made with it can be frozen filled or unfilled.

Store pastries in an airtight container. If they contain fresh cream store in the refrigerator or cold larder if necessary – but they are best eaten as soon as possible.

Shortcrust pastry; Macaroon mincemeat tarts

Shortcrust pastry

Metric	Imperial
200 g plain flour	8 oz plain flour
Pinch of salt	Pinch of salt
100 g fat (butter, margarine or a mixture of margarine and lard or cooking fat)	4 oz fat (butter, margarine or a mixture of margarine and lard or cooking fat)
About 3 × 15 ml spoons water	About 3 tablespoons water

Sieve together the flour and salt. Cut the fat into small pieces and rub lightly into the flour, using your fingertips, until the mixture resembles fine breadcrumbs. Add the water and bind the mixture, using a knife, so that it clings together leaving the sides of the bowl clean. Place on a floured working surface or board and knead very lightly to a smooth round ball. Roll out the pastry and use as required.

Note: When a recipe states 100 g (4 oz) shortcrust pastry it means pastry made with 100 g (4 oz) flour and 50 g (2 oz) fat. For sweet shortcrust pastry add 25 g (1 oz) caster sugar.

Macaroon mincemeat tarts

Metric	Imperial
150 g shortcrust pastry (see above)	6 oz shortcrust pastry (see above)
4 × 15 ml spoons mincemeat	4 tablespoons mincemeat
2 standard egg whites	2 large egg whites
75 g caster sugar	3 oz caster sugar
75 g ground almonds	3 oz ground almonds
15 g flaked almonds	½ oz flaked almonds
Few glacé cherries, quartered	Few glacé cherries, quartered

Cooking Time: 20 minutes
Oven: 190°C, 375°F, Gas Mark 5

Roll out the pastry, cut into 8 cm (3 in) circles and use to line 10–12 patty tins. Divide the mincemeat between the pastry cases. Whisk the egg whites until they are stiff. Fold in the sugar and almonds. Pile the macaroon mixture on top of the mincemeat and sprinkle with the flaked almonds. Place a quartered cherry in the centre of each tart. Bake in a moderately hot oven for 20 minutes or until golden brown.

Makes 10–12

Treacle tart

Treacle tart

Metric	*Imperial*
150 g shortcrust pastry	*6 oz shortcrust pastry*
(page 75)	*(page 75)*
50 g fresh white	*2 oz fresh white*
breadcrumbs	*breadcrumbs*
200 g golden syrup	*8 oz golden syrup*
2 × 5 ml spoons finely	*2 teaspoons finely*
grated lemon rind	*grated lemon rind*

Cooking Time: 25–30 minutes
Oven: 200°C, 400°F, Gas Mark 6

Roll out the pastry and use to line a 20 cm (8 in) pie plate. Stir the breadcrumbs into the syrup and add the lemon rind. Turn into the pie dish. Roll out the pastry trimmings and cut into thin strips for a lattice. Place in position, damping the pastry well so that the lattice sticks. Bake in a moderately hot oven for 25–30 minutes or until the pastry is pale golden. Allow to cool.

Coconut meringue slices

Metric	*Imperial*
200 g shortcrust pastry	*8 oz shortcrust pastry*
(page 75)	*(page 75)*
3 × 15 ml spoons	*3 tablespoons*
raspberry jam	*raspberry jam*
2 standard egg whites	*2 large egg whites*
100 g caster sugar	*4 oz caster sugar*
100 g desiccated coconut	*4 oz desiccated coconut*

Cooking Time: 30 minutes
Oven: 180°C, 350°F, Gas Mark 4

Grease an 18 × 28 cm (7 × 11 in) swiss roll tin. Roll out the pastry and line the base and sides of the tin. Spread with the jam. Whisk the egg whites until they stand in stiff peaks. Gradually whisk in half the sugar a teaspoonful at a time. Fold in the remaining sugar and most of the coconut. Spoon on top of the jam and spread carefully with a palette knife. Bake in a moderate oven for about 15 minutes. Sprinkle with the remaining coconut and return to the oven until the top is golden. Allow to cool in the tin and cut into fingers while still warm.
Makes 14 fingers

Spiced curd tarts; Coconut meringue slices

Spiced curd tarts

Metric	Imperial
200 g shortcrust pastry (page 75)	8 oz shortcrust pastry (page 75)
50 g stoned or seedless raisins	2 oz stoned or seedless raisins
50 g butter	2 oz butter
50 g caster sugar	2 oz caster sugar
1 × 5 ml spoon finely grated lemon rind	1 teaspoon finely grated lemon rind
1 standard egg, lightly beaten	1 large egg, lightly beaten
1 × 15 ml spoon self-raising flour	1 tablespoon self-raising flour
½ teaspoon ground cinnamon	½ teaspoon ground cinnamon
200 g curd cheese	8 oz curd cheese
2 × 15 ml spoons milk	2 tablespoons milk

Cooking Time: 30 minutes
Oven: 180°C, 350°F, Gas Mark 4

Roll out the pastry, cut into 8 cm (3 in) circles with a fluted cutter and use to line 14–16 patty tins. Lightly prick the pastry and put a few raisins in the bottom of each tart. Cream the butter, sugar and lemon rind until soft and light. Gradually beat in the egg, then the flour sieved with the cinnamon, the cheese and the milk. Divide the mixture between the pastry cases. Bake in a moderate oven for about 30 minutes or until the filling is well risen and set.
Makes 14–16

77

Duke of cambridge tart

Metric	Imperial
100 g shortcrust pastry (page 75)	4 oz shortcrust pastry (page 75)
25 g glacé cherries, chopped	1 oz glacé cherries, chopped
25 g angelica, chopped	1 oz angelica, chopped
25 g chopped mixed peel	1 oz chopped mixed peel
2 eggs	2 eggs
1 × 15 ml spoon caster sugar	1 tablespoon caster sugar
250 ml milk	½ pint milk

Cooking Time: 50 minutes
Oven: 190°C, 375°F, Gas Mark 5

Roll out the pastry and use to line an 18 cm (7 in) fluted flan ring. Prick the bottom of the pastry, line with greaseproof paper, fill with baking beans and bake blind for 10 minutes. Remove the greaseproof paper and beans and bake for a further 5 minutes.

Mix the cherries, angelica and peel together and sprinkle over the base of the flan. Beat the eggs and sugar, pour in the milk and blend well. Strain over the mixed fruit. Bake in a moderately hot oven for about 35 minutes or until the custard has set. Remove the flan ring and cool before serving.

Linzertorte

Metric	Imperial
150 g plain flour	6 oz plain flour
½ teaspoon ground cinnamon	½ teaspoon ground cinnamon
75 g butter	3 oz butter
50 g sugar	2 oz sugar
50 g ground almonds	2 oz ground almonds
2 × 5 ml spoons finely grated lemon rind	2 teaspoons finely grated lemon rind
2 standard egg yolks	2 large egg yolks
About 1 × 15 ml spoon lemon juice	About 1 tablespoon lemon juice
300 g raspberry jam	12 oz raspberry jam

Cooking Time: 25–30 minutes
Oven: 190°C, 375°F, Gas Mark 5

Sift the flour and cinnamon into a bowl. Rub in the butter until the mixture resembles fine breadcrumbs. Add the sugar, almonds and lemon rind. Bind the pastry with the egg yolks and enough lemon juice to make a stiff dough. Turn the dough on to a floured surface and knead lightly. Roll two thirds of the dough out and use to line an 18–20 cm (7–8 in) fluted flan ring on a baking tray. Make sure the dough is evenly rolled out, press to the shape of the ring and trim off the excess pastry. Fill the flan with the raspberry jam. Roll out the reserved pastry and trimmings and cut into strips with a pastry wheel or knife. Use these to make a lattice over the jam. Bake in a moderately hot oven for 25–30 minutes until golden brown. Allow to cool, then remove the flan ring.

Heavenly favours

Metric	Imperial
For the dough:	For the dough:
200 g plain flour	8 oz plain flour
¼ teaspoon salt	¼ teaspoon salt
25 g lard	1 oz lard
25 g margarine	1 oz margarine
2 standard eggs, lightly beaten	2 large eggs, lightly beaten
1–2 × 15 ml spoons milk	1–2 tablespoons milk
Deep oil or fat for frying	Deep oil or fat for frying
To serve:	To serve:
Caster sugar	Caster sugar
Ground cinnamon	Ground cinnamon
Jam	Jam

Cooking Time: about 3–5 minutes

Sieve the flour and salt. Rub in the lard and margarine. Add the eggs and milk and mix to a soft dough. Turn on to a lightly-floured surface and knead for about 5 minutes until the mixture is smooth. Cover the dough and leave in a warm place for 1 hour. Place the dough on a floured surface and roll out to a rectangle. Fold the top third down and the bottom third up like an envelope, and give the dough a half turn. Repeat this twice and leave the dough to rest for 10 minutes. Roll out the dough until it is 6 mm (¼ in) thick and cut into diamonds. Heat the fat until a cube of bread browns in 40–50 seconds and fry the pastry diamonds until they are golden brown. Remove from the fat and drain, sprinkle with sugar and cinnamon and serve with jam while still warm.
Makes about 18

Fruit-filled boats; Duke of Cambridge tart; Linzertorte; Heavenly favours

Fruit-filled boats

Metric

For the pastry:
150 g plain flour
Pinch of salt
75 g butter or margarine
25 g caster sugar
1 standard egg yolk
A very little water

For the filling:
200 g fresh or canned fruit
(cherries, strawberries,
raspberries, mandarins etc)
4 × 15 ml spoons
redcurrant jelly
1 × 15 ml spoon fruit juice
125 ml double cream,
lightly whipped

Imperial

For the pastry:
6 oz plain flour
Pinch of salt
3 oz butter or margarine
1 oz caster sugar
1 large egg yolk
A very little water

For the filling:
8 oz fresh or canned fruit
(cherries, strawberries,
raspberries, mandarins etc)
4 tablespoons
redcurrant jelly
1 tablespoon fruit juice
¼ pint double cream,
lightly whipped

Cooking Time: 10 minutes
Oven: 190°C, 375°F, Gas Mark 5

Sieve together the flour and salt. Rub in the butter or margarine until the mixture resembles fine breadcrumbs. Add the sugar and bind with the egg yolk and water to a stiff dough. Turn on to a floured surface and knead very lightly. Use the pastry to line 12 boat tins about 10 × 5 cm (4 × 2 in). Prick the sides and bases and bake blind in a moderately hot oven for 10 minutes. Allow to cool and remove from the tins.

Arrange the fruit attractively in the pastry cases. Melt the jelly with the fruit juice over a very low heat and brush over the fruit; if you are using an orange fruit, such as mandarins, you may prefer to use sieved apricot jam. Leave until the glaze is quite cold. Spoon the cream into a piping bag with a small rose nozzle and use to decorate the boats.
Makes 12

Puff pastry

Puff pastry

Metric	*Imperial*
200 g plain flour	*8 oz plain flour*
½ teaspoon salt	*½ teaspoon salt*
1 × 5 ml spoon lemon juice	*1 teaspoon lemon juice*
About 125 ml water	*About ¼ pint water*
200 g butter	*8 oz butter*

Sieve together the flour and salt. Add the lemon juice and enough water to mix to a soft dough. Soften the butter and reform into an oblong. Roll out the dough to a rectangle about 30 × 20 cm (12 × 8 in) and place the butter in the centre. Fold the ends to the centre, like a parcel, to cover the butter, press the centre edges and sides to seal.

Turn the pastry a quarter of a circle and roll out to a rectangle again. Mark the dough into three and fold the lower third up and the top third down, like an envelope. Seal the edges. Put the dough into a polythene bag and leave to rest in the refrigerator for at least 10 minutes. Take the dough out of the bag, give it a half turn and repeat the rolling and folding 6 times, allowing it to rest in the refrigerator for 10 minutes every second rolling. Refrigerate for 1 hour before using.

Note : When a recipe states 100 g (4 oz) puff pastry it means pastry made with 100 g (4 oz) flour and 100 g (4 oz) butter.

Apple strudel

Metric

For the dough:
200 g plain flour
½ teaspoon salt
1 standard egg, lightly beaten
2 × 15 ml spoons oil
3 × 15 ml spoons warm water

For the filling:
100 g butter
50 g fresh white breadcrumbs
600 g cooking apples, peeled, cored and coarsely grated
50 g raisins
50 g currants
75 g caster sugar
½ teaspoon ground cinnamon
2 × 5 ml spoons finely grated lemon rind

To serve:
Icing sugar, sieved

Imperial

For the dough:
8 oz plain flour
½ teaspoon salt
1 large egg, lightly beaten
2 tablespoons oil
3 tablespoons warm water

For the filling:
4 oz butter
2 oz fresh white breadcrumbs
1½ lb cooking apples, peeled, cored and coarsely grated
2 oz raisins
2 oz currants
3 oz caster sugar
½ teaspoon ground cinnamon
2 teaspoons finely grated lemon rind

To serve:
Icing sugar, sieved

Cooking Time: 50 minutes
Oven: 200°C, 400°F, Gas Mark 6;
    180°C, 350°F, Gas Mark 4

Sieve together the flour and salt. Make a well in the centre and pour in the egg and oil. Add the water gradually, stirring with a fork, to make a soft sticky dough. Work the dough in the bowl until it leaves the sides clean, then turn out on to a lightly-floured surface and knead for about 15 minutes or until the dough feels smooth and elastic. Form into a ball, place in a bowl and cover with a warm cloth. Leave to rest for 1 hour.

Melt half the butter in a pan and fry the breadcrumbs until they are crisp and golden. Add the apples, raisins, currants, sugar, cinnamon and lemon rind.

Warm the rolling pin, and flour a large clean tea towel. Place the dough on the towel and roll it out to a rectangle as thin as possible, lifting and turning it to prevent it from sticking to the cloth. Using the backs of your hands, gently stretch the dough, working from the centre to the outside until it is paper thin – you should be able to read through the dough, but to do this takes years of practice and patience. Leave the dough to rest for 15 minutes.

Melt the remaining butter and use most of it to brush all over the dough. Spread the filling on the dough to within 2.5 cm (1 in) of the edges. Lift the two corners of the tea towel nearest to you and roll the dough away from you. Place the dough on a greased baking sheet and form into a horseshoe. Brush all over with the remaining melted butter. Bake in a moderately hot oven for about 20 minutes, then lower heat for a further 30 minutes. Serve warm or cold. Dust with icing sugar and cut into slices.

Apple strudel

Jamaican puffs

Metric	Imperial
100 g puff pastry or use a 212 g packet frozen puff pastry, thawed	*4 oz puff pastry or use a 7½ oz packet frozen puff pastry, thawed*
2 bananas, peeled and sliced	*2 bananas, peeled and sliced*
2 × 5 ml spoons lemon juice	*2 teaspoons lemon juice*
250 ml double cream, stiffly whipped	*½ pint double cream, stiffly whipped*
2 × 15 ml spoons rum (optional)	*2 tablespoons rum (optional)*
25 g hazelnuts, finely chopped	*1 oz hazelnuts, finely chopped*
Icing sugar for dusting	*Icing sugar for dusting*

Cooking Time: 10 minutes
Oven: 220°C, 425°F, Gas Mark 8

Roll the pastry out to a 23 cm (9 in) square. Trim the edges, then cut into 9 × 8 cm (3 in) squares. Place the squares on a damp baking sheet and bake in a hot oven for 10 minutes. Cool on a wire rack.

Toss the bananas lightly in the lemon juice. Fold the rum, if using, into the cream. Carefully split the pastry squares in half, using a small sharp knife. Pipe the bottom half of each pastry with the cream, sprinkle with the hazelnuts and top with slices of banana. Replace the lids and dust with icing sugar before serving.
Makes 9

Mincemeat and apple fingers

Metric	Imperial
For the pastry:	For the pastry:
200 g plain flour	*8 oz plain flour*
Pinch of salt	*Pinch of salt*
75 g lard	*3 oz lard*
75 g margarine	*3 oz margarine*
About 125 ml cold water	*About ¼ pint cold water*
For the filling:	For the filling:
1 large or 2 medium-sized cooking apples, peeled, cored and grated	*1 large or 2 medium-sized cooking apples, peeled, cored and grated*
300 g mincemeat	*12 oz mincemeat*
To glaze:	To glaze:
A little milk	*A little milk*

Cooking Time: 25–30 minutes
Oven: 220°C, 425°F, Gas Mark 7

Sieve the flour and salt into a bowl. Add the lard and margarine and cut the fat up roughly into small pieces about 1.5 cm (½ in) square, using two round-bladed knives in a scissor action. Add the water and mix to a soft dough. Turn on to a floured surface and roll out to a rectangle about 13 × 30 cm (5 × 12 in). Bring the top third of the dough down and the bottom third up to make an envelope shape. Turn the dough so the fold is on the right-hand side and repeat the rolling and folding three more times. Wrap in a piece of foil or greaseproof paper and rest in the refrigerator for 30 minutes before rolling out.

Divide the pastry in half and roll out two rectangles about 20 × 30 cm (8 × 12 in). Place one on a damp baking sheet. Stir the grated apple into the mincemeat and spread this on the pastry to within 1.5 cm (½ in) of the edges. Damp the pastry edges with water and place the second rectangle on top. Press the edges well together to seal and knock up with the back of a knife. Brush all over the pastry with milk and bake in a hot oven for 25–30 minutes. Cut into squares or fingers and serve either warm or cold.

French cream twists

Metric	Imperial
200 g puff pastry (page 80) or use a 368 g packet frozen puff pastry, thawed	*8 oz puff pastry (page 80) or use a 13 oz packet frozen puff pastry, thawed*
For the glaze:	For the glaze:
1 egg white	*1 egg white*
For the filling:	For the filling:
4 × 15 ml spoons strawberry jam	*4 tablespoons strawberry jam*
125 ml double cream, lightly whipped	*¼ pint double cream, lightly whipped*
To serve:	To serve:
Icing sugar, sieved	*Icing sugar, sieved*

Cooking Time: 10 minutes
Oven: 230°C, 450°F, Gas Mark 8

Roll the pastry out to a 30 cm (12 in) square and trim the edges. Cut into 24 strips by dividing into 3 one way and 8 the other. Lay half the strips on a damp baking sheet. Holding either end of the other strips, twist once and place on a second damp baking sheet. Lightly whisk the egg white with a fork and brush each pastry strip with it. Allow the pastry to rest for 15 minutes before baking.

Bake in a very hot oven for 10 minutes or until golden brown. Allow to cool on the baking sheets. When the pastries are quite cold pipe a layer of cream on the flat strips and spread with jam. Place the twists of pastry on top and spinkle with sieved icing sugar before serving.
Makes 12

Baklava

Metric	Imperial
50 g butter	*2 oz butter*
3 × 15 ml spoons clear honey	*3 tablespoons clear honey*
½ teaspoon ground cinnamon	*½ teaspoon ground cinnamon*
150 g blanched almonds, finely chopped	*6 oz blanched almonds, finely chopped*
200 g puff pastry (page 80) or use a 368 g packet frozen puff pastry, thawed	*8 oz puff pastry (page 80) or use a 13 oz packet frozen puff pastry, thawed*
200 g sugar	*8 oz sugar*
250 ml water	*½ pint water*
1 × 15 ml spoon lemon juice	*1 tablespoon lemon juice*

Cooking Time: 20 minutes
Oven: 200°C, 400°F, Gas Mark 6

Cream the butter, 1 × 15 ml spoon (1 tablespoon) of the honey and the cinnamon together. Stir in the chopped almonds. Roll out the pastry and cut out 4 × 15 cm (6 in) squares. Cover a baking sheet with foil. Place one piece of pastry on it and spread with one third of the almond mixture. Top with another pastry square and repeat these layers, finishing with a square of pastry. Mark the top layer into 5 cm (2 in) diamonds with a sharp knife. Bake in a moderately hot oven for 20 minutes or until the top is golden brown.

While the pastry is cooking put the sugar, water, lemon juice and remaining honey into a saucepan. Heat slowly until the sugar has dissolved, then simmer for 5 minutes. Remove the baking tray from the oven and pull up the foil on the tray to form a case around the sides of the pastry. Pour the hot syrup over and leave to soak for about 6 hours. When cold, cut into diamonds.

Mincemeat and apple fingers; Baklava; Jamaican puffs; French cream twists

Choux pastry

Metric	Imperial
65 g plain flour	2½ oz plain flour
Pinch of salt	Pinch of salt
50 g butter or margarine	2 oz butter or margarine
100 ml water	¼ pint water
1 × 5 ml spoon sugar	1 teaspoon sugar
2 standard eggs	2 standard eggs
1 egg yolk	1 egg yolk

Sieve together the flour and salt. Put the butter or margarine, cut into small pieces, into a pan with the water and sugar. Bring slowly to the boil. Remove from the heat and add the flour all at once. Beat well until the mixture forms a soft ball that leaves the sides of the pan clean; if necessary return to a very gentle heat. Allow the mixture to cool for 5 minutes. Beat in the whole eggs, one at a time, then the egg yolk, until the mixture is smooth and shiny.

Note : If a recipe states 65 g (2½ oz) choux pastry it means pastry made with 65 g (2½ oz) flour, 50 g (2 oz) butter or margarine.

Choux swans

Metric	Imperial
65 g choux pastry (see above)	2½ oz choux pastry (see above)
250 ml double cream, lightly whipped	½ pint double cream, lightly whipped
Icing sugar, sieved	Icing sugar, sieved

Cooking Time: 25 minutes
Oven: 200°C, 400°F, Gas Mark 6

Make up the choux pastry and spoon most of it into a piping bag fitted with a 1.5 cm (½ in) plain nozzle. Pipe out 20 small buns on one or two greased baking sheets, allowing plenty of room for them to spread. Spoon the remaining pastry into a bag fitted with a 6 mm (¼ in) plain nozzle and pipe out 20 S-shapes on a greased baking sheet for the swans' necks. Bake the buns for about 25 minutes in a moderately hot oven and the necks for 10–15 minutes. Cool the buns and necks on a wire rack.

Split each bun in half and cut the top half of each bun in half again for the wings. Pipe a whirl of cream on the base of each bun and fix the wings and neck into position. Dust with sieved icing sugar before serving.
Makes 20

Choux swans

Cream buns

Metric	Imperial
65 g choux pastry *(see opposite)*	*2½ oz choux pastry* *(see opposite)*

For the filling:
1 standard egg white
125 ml double cream, lightly whipped
1 × 15 ml spoon caster sugar

For the filling:
1 large egg white
¼ pint double cream, lightly whipped
1 tablespoon caster sugar

For the icing:
100 g plain chocolate

For the icing:
4 oz plain chocolate

Cooking Time: 40–45 minutes
Oven: 200°C, 400°F, Gas Mark 6;
    180°C, 350°F, Gas Mark 4

Make up the choux pastry and place in 8–10 tablespoonfuls on one or two greased baking sheets, allowing plenty of room for them to spread. Bake in a moderately hot oven for 20 minutes, then reduce the heat and bake for a further 15 minutes. Remove the buns from the oven, make a slit in them to allow the steam to escape and replace for a further 5–10 minutes to dry out. Remove from the oven and cool on a wire rack.

Whisk the egg white until it forms stiff peaks. Fold into the cream with the sugar. Split each bun almost in half and divide the cream between them. Break the chocolate into pieces and put into a basin over a pan of hot water. When the chocolate has melted spoon some carefully over the top of each bun.
Makes 8–10

Cream buns

Home-made biscuits and cookies are a marvellous standby for the storecupboard as they will keep well for at least a week in an airtight container.
All the biscuits given here are very simple to make and many of them are based on a shortbread mixture. The basic shortbread recipe can also be varied in many different ways, by adding finely grated orange or lemon rind, dried fruit etc.
Baked home-made biscuits can also be frozen. The dough for the Orange Refrigerator Cookies can be put into the deep-freeze rather than storing it in the refrigerator. If you do this, you may prefer to cut the dough into four before freezing, so that you can bake about a dozen cookies at one time.

Shortbread wheels

Metric	Imperial
125 g plain flour	*5 oz plain flour*
50 g caster sugar	*2 oz caster sugar*
100 g butter	*4 oz butter*
1 × 15 ml spoon cocoa powder	*1 tablespoon cocoa powder*
1 × 15 ml spoon drinking chocolate powder	*1 tablespoon drinking chocolate powder*

Cooking Time: 12 minutes
Oven: 180°C, 350°F, Gas Mark 4

Sieve 110 g (4½ oz) of the flour into a bowl. Add the sugar. Rub in the butter until it is crumbly and divide the mixture in half. Add the remaining flour to one half and the cocoa and drinking chocolate to the other half. Knead each portion well with your fingers to form a smooth dough. Turn on to a board or working surface lightly dusted with flour or cornflour. Roll out each portion to 6 mm (¼ in) thick and from each cut out 7 × 6 cm (2½ in) circles. Out of these circles cut two more circles, one 4 cm (1½ in) and one 2 cm (¾ in), making three in all.
Separate these circles and place on greased baking sheets, alternating the colours so that in half the biscuits you have two plain and one chocolate circle and in the others you have two chocolate and one plain circle. Bake in a moderate oven for 12 minutes. Leave on the sheets for 2 minutes, then remove with a palette knife and cool on a wire rack.
Makes 14
Note : If preferred simply roll out the dough to 2 rectangles and place one on top of the other. Roll up like a swiss roll, cut into thin slices and place on greased baking sheets.

Butter shortbread

Metric	Imperial
100 g plain flour	*4 oz plain flour*
50 g cornflour	*2 oz cornflour*
50 g caster sugar	*2 oz caster sugar*
100 g butter	*4 oz butter*

Cooking Time: 30–35 minutes
Oven: 170°C, 325°F, Gas Mark 3

Sieve together the flour and cornflour. Add the sugar. Rub in the butter. The mixture will become crumbly at first, but continue rubbing in with your fingers until it clings together in heavy lumps. Turn on to a board or working surface lightly dusted with flour or cornflour and knead lightly. Roll out to a 20 cm (8 in) circle and place on a greased baking sheet. Prick all over the top with a fork, mark into 8–10 portions and flute the edges with your fingers. Bake in a very moderate oven for 30–35 minutes until the shortbread is cooked but not browned. Leave on the baking tray for 10 minutes, then lift off with a fish slice and place carefully on a wire rack to cool.

Shortbread wheels; Butter shortbread

Peanut cookies

Metric	Imperial
100 g butter or margarine	4 oz butter or margarine
50 g caster sugar	2 oz caster sugar
150 g plain flour	6 oz plain flour
Pinch of salt	Pinch of salt
A little milk	A little milk
50 g peanuts, roughly chopped	2 oz peanuts, roughly chopped

Cooking Time: 12 minutes
Oven: 180°C, 350°F, Gas Mark 4

Cream the butter or margarine and sugar until light and fluffy. Sieve the flour and salt, stir into the mixture and mix to a stiff dough. Turn on to a floured surface, knead lightly and roll out 6 mm ($\frac{1}{4}$ in) thick. Cut into circles with a 5 cm (2 in) cutter and place on greased baking sheets. Brush the biscuits with milk and sprinkle with the chopped nuts. Bake in a moderate oven for about 12 minutes or until crisp and golden brown. Leave on the sheets for a minute, then remove and cool on a wire rack.
Makes about 20

Date pinwheel cookies

Metric	Imperial
For the filling:	For the filling:
100 g dates, stoned and chopped	4 oz dates, stoned and chopped
75 g caster sugar	3 oz caster sugar
125 ml water	$\frac{1}{4}$ pint water
25 g blanched almonds, finely chopped	1 oz blanched almonds, finely chopped
For the shortbread:	For the shortbread:
100 g self-raising flour	4 oz self-raising flour
$\frac{1}{4}$ teaspoon salt	$\frac{1}{4}$ teaspoon salt
$\frac{1}{4}$ teaspoon baking powder	$\frac{1}{4}$ teaspoon baking powder
50 g butter	2 oz butter
75 g caster sugar	3 oz caster sugar
1 standard egg yolk	1 large egg yolk

Cooking Time: 10–12 minutes
Oven: 190°C, 375°F, Gas Mark 5

Put the dates into a pan with the sugar and the water. Simmer gently over a low heat until the mixture becomes thick. Remove from the heat, cool, then stir in the almonds. Sieve the flour, salt and baking powder. Cream the butter and sugar until light and fluffy. Beat in the egg yolk, then stir in the flour. Knead to a smooth dough, wrap in grease-proof paper or foil and chill for 1 hour.
Roll out the dough on a lightly-floured surface to a rectangle about 20 × 35 cm (8 × 14 in). Spoon the date mixture over it and spread into an even layer with a palette knife. Roll up the dough like a swiss roll but starting at a short side. Wrap in greaseproof paper or foil and chill in the refrigerator for 3–4 hours.
Cut the roll into 6 mm ($\frac{1}{4}$ in) thick slices, using a sharp knife, and place the slices on well-greased baking sheets, allowing room for the cookies to spread. Bake in a moderately hot oven for 10–12 minutes or until golden. Leave on the trays for a minute then remove with a palette knife and cool on a wire rack.
Makes about 30

Cinnamon and almond slices

Metric	Imperial
100 g butter	4 oz butter
50 g caster sugar	2 oz caster sugar
150 g plain flour	6 oz plain flour
$\frac{1}{2}$ teaspoon ground cinnamon	$\frac{1}{2}$ teaspoon ground cinnamon
A little beaten egg for glazing	A little beaten egg for glazing
25 g flaked almonds	1 oz flaked almonds
1 × 15 ml spoon granulated sugar	1 tablespoon granulated sugar

Cooking Time: 20 minutes
Oven: 180°C, 350°F, Gas Mark 4

Well grease a 28 × 18 cm (11 × 7 in) swiss roll tin. Cream the butter and sugar together until light and fluffy. Sieve in the flour and cinnamon and work well together. Press into the prepared tin and flatten with a palette knife. Brush with a little beaten egg and prick with a fork. Sprinkle over the almonds and sugar. Bake in a moderate oven for 20 minutes or until golden brown. Cool in the tin and mark into 18 fingers while still warm.
Makes 18 fingers

Peanut cookies; Cinnamon and almond slices; Date pinwheel cookies

Orange refrigerator cookies

Metric	Imperial
250 g plain flour	10 oz plain flour
1 × 5 ml spoon baking powder	1 teaspoon baking powder
125 g butter or margarine	5 oz butter or margarine
150 g caster sugar	6 oz caster sugar
2 × 5 ml spoons finely grated orange rind	2 teaspoons finely grated orange rind
1 standard egg, lightly beaten	1 large egg, lightly beaten
50 g currants	2 oz currants
Extra caster sugar for dusting	Extra caster sugar for dusting

Cooking Time: about 15 minutes
Oven: 180°C, 350°F, Gas Mark 4

The dough for these cookies can be kept in the refrigerator well-wrapped, for a week. Simply slice off and bake as many biscuits as you require.

Sieve together the flour and baking powder. Cream the butter or margarine, sugar and orange rind until light and fluffy. Beat in the egg. Stir in the currants and the flour until the mixture clings together. Turn on to a lightly-floured surface and form into a sausage shape with your hands about 5 cm (2 in) in diameter. Wrap in foil or waxed paper and chill in the refrigerator for at least 2 hours.

To cook the biscuits thinly slice off as many as you need and place on greased baking sheets. Sprinkle with sugar and bake in a moderate oven for about 15 minutes. Cool on the sheets for 2 minutes, then transfer to a wire rack.

Makes about 48

Bourbon biscuits

Metric	Imperial
100 g plain flour	4 oz plain flour
½ teaspoon baking powder	½ teaspoon baking powder
15 g cocoa powder	½ oz cocoa powder
50 g margarine	2 oz margarine
50 g caster sugar	2 oz caster sugar
1 × 15 ml spoon golden syrup	1 tablespoon golden syrup
For the filling:	For the filling:
25 g plain chocolate	1 oz plain chocolate
1½ × 15 ml spoons water	1½ tablespoons water
50 g icing sugar, sieved	2 oz icing sugar, sieved

Cooking Time: 15–20 minutes
Oven: 170°C, 325°F, Gas Mark 3

Sieve together the flour, baking powder and cocoa. Cream the margarine and sugar until light and fluffy. Beat in the syrup. Stir in half the flour and cocoa and mix until smooth. Turn the dough on to a working surface and knead in the remaining flour. Roll the dough out thinly on a very lightly floured surface. Cut into fingers about 2.5 cm (1 in) wide by 6 cm (2½ in) long. Lift carefully on to well-greased baking sheets with a palette knife. Prick the biscuits with a fork and bake in a slow oven for 15–20 minutes or until crisp. Remove from the sheets and cool on a wire rack.

Put the chocolate and water into a small pan. Place over a very gentle heat until the chocolate has melted. Remove from the heat and beat in the icing sugar to give a thick, glossy icing. Cool until the mixture is of a spreading consistency, then spread over half the biscuits and sandwich the remaining biscuits on top.

Makes about 15

Bourbon biscuits; Orange refrigerator cookies

Nutty rolls

Nutty rolls

Metric

For the wafers:
75 g golden syrup
50 g butter
50 g dark brown sugar
65 g self-raising flour
40 g walnuts, finely
chopped

For the filling:
125 ml double cream
½ teaspoon instant coffee
powder
25 g icing sugar, sieved

Imperial

For the wafers:
3 oz golden syrup
2 oz butter
2 oz dark brown sugar
2½ oz self-raising flour
1½ oz walnuts, finely
chopped

For the filling:
¼ pint double cream
½ teaspoon instant coffee
powder
1 oz icing sugar, sieved

Cooking Time: 6 minutes
Oven: 190°C, 375°F, Gas Mark 5

Line greased baking sheets with non-stick silicone paper. Oil the handles of 4 wooden spoons. Put the syrup, butter and sugar into a saucepan over a low heat until the butter has melted and the sugar dissolved. Remove from the heat and beat in the sieved flour and walnuts. Put teaspoons of the mixture on the baking sheets, about 8 cm (3 in) apart. Bake in a moderately hot oven for 6 minutes. Allow to cool on the sheets for a few minutes. Lift off with a palette knife and roll round the handle of a wooden spoon. Allow to set and repeat with the remaining biscuits. Bake the biscuits in batches so that you have plenty of time to roll them. If they do become too hard, replace in the oven for a few minutes to soften.

Just before serving whip the cream with the coffee and icing sugar. Put into a piping bag with a large rose nozzle and pipe into the biscuits.

Makes about 20

Oatmeal and chocolate chip cookies

Metric	Imperial
100 g butter or margarine	4 oz butter or margarine
100 g caster sugar	4 oz caster sugar
1 standard egg, beaten	1 large egg, beaten
½ teaspoon vanilla essence	½ teaspoon vanilla essence
75 g plain flour	3 oz plain flour
Pinch of salt	Pinch of salt
40 g rolled oats	1½ oz rolled oats
100 g chocolate chips	4 oz chocolate chips

Cooking Time: 12–15 minutes
Oven: 180°C, 350°F, Gas Mark 4

Cream the butter or margarine and sugar together until light and fluffy. Gradually beat in the egg and vanilla essence. Sieve in the flour and salt. Fold into the creamed mixture together with the oats and chocolate chips.

Put teaspoons of the mixture on to very well-greased baking sheets; you will probably have to bake the biscuits in two batches. Bake in a moderate oven for 12–15 minutes or until very lightly browned. Leave on the baking trays for a minute, then remove from the trays with a palette knife and cool on wire racks.

Makes about 36

Anzac cookies

Metric	Imperial
2 × 15 ml spoons golden syrup	2 tablespoons golden syrup
125 g butter	5 oz butter
100 g caster sugar	4 oz caster sugar
100 g plain flour	4 oz plain flour
75 g rolled oats	3 oz rolled oats
50 g desiccated coconut	2 oz desiccated coconut
2 × 5 ml spoons bicarbonate of soda	2 teaspoons bicarbonate of soda
1 × 15 ml spoon hot water	1 tablespoon hot water

Cooking Time: 20 minutes
Oven: 170°C, 325°F, Gas Mark 3

Put the syrup, butter and sugar into a saucepan and heat gently until the butter has melted and the sugar dissolved. Remove from the heat, sieve in the flour, add the oats and coconut and beat well. Dissolve the bicarbonate of soda in the water and add to the mixture in the pan. When the mixture is cool enough to handle, roll into about 30 small balls and place on greased baking sheets, allowing plenty of room for the cookies to spread.

Bake in a very moderate oven for 20 minutes or until the cookies are an even golden brown. Leave on the baking trays for a minute or two to harden, then place on wire racks to cool.

Makes about 30

Brown biscuits

Metric	Imperial
100 g butter	4 oz butter
100 g caster sugar	4 oz caster sugar
50 g golden syrup	2 oz golden syrup
25 g blanched almonds, finely chopped	1 oz blanched almonds, finely chopped
25 g chopped mixed peel	1 oz chopped mixed peel
200 g plain flour	8 oz plain flour
½ teaspoon ground cloves	½ teaspoon ground cloves
1 × 5 ml spoon ground cinnamon	1 teaspoon ground cinnamon
¼ teaspoon ground ginger	¼ teaspoon ground ginger

Cooking Time: 10 minutes
Oven: 200°C, 400°F, Gas Mark 6

Put the butter, sugar and syrup into a pan and heat gently until the butter has melted and the sugar dissolved. Remove from the heat and add the almonds and peel. Allow to cool, then sieve in the flour with the spices. Mix well. Using your hands, roll the dough into a sausage about 6 cm (2½ in) in diameter. Wrap in greaseproof paper and put into the refrigerator for a few hours or overnight.

Remove the greaseproof paper and cut the dough into paper-thin slices. Place on greased baking sheets and bake in a moderately hot oven for 10 minutes or until crisp. Leave on the baking sheets a minute, then remove with a palette knife and cool on a wire rack.

Makes about 36